Jesmond

from mines to mansions

St George's Church and vicarage c1888.

Jesmond

from mines to mansions

Brandling Park, Newcastle-on-Tyne

Alan Morgan

Tyne Bridge Publishing

Acknowledgements

This book is dedicated to the memory of Jimmy Donald, whose love of local history was an inspiration.

Our grateful thanks to Chris Donald for making available his father's papers on the history of Jesmond, and for writing the foreword to **Jesmond from mines to mansions**.

Many sources were consulted in the preparation of this book but particularly helpful were *Bygone Jesmond* (1987) and *Not Just Bricks and Mortar* (1994) both by Jimmy Donald; *An Account of Jesmond* by F.W. Dendy (1904); *West Jesmond School* by Christine Jeans (2002); *Coals from Newcastle* by Les Turnbull (2009).

Bygone Jesmond Dene by Alan Morgan extends the information in this book to cover Jesmond Dene.

Unless otherwise indicated the photographs in this book are part of the Local Studies collection at Newcastle Libraries and are ©Newcastle Libraries.

Other books by Alan Morgan from Tyne Bridge Publishing

Beyond the Grave: Newcastle's Burial Grounds Explored
Bygone Jesmond Dene
Bygone Jesmond Vale
Bygone Lower Ouseburn
Bygone Sandyford and Cradlewell
Bygone Shieldfield
A Fine and Private Place: Jesmond Old Cemetery
Victorian Panorama: A visit to Newcastle upon Tyne in the Reign of Queen Victoria

Tyne Bridge Publishing
Newcastle Libraries
PO Box 88
Newcastle upon Tyne
NE99 1DX
Tel: 0191 277 4174
www.tynebridgepublishing.co.uk

©Alan Morgan, 2010
ISBN 978 185795 200 1
Published by
City of Newcastle upon Tyne
Newcastle Libraries
Tyne Bridge Publishing
2010
www.newcastle.gov.uk/libraries

Printed by Elanders, North Tyneside

Foreword - Remembering Jimmy Donald

A lot of historians are obsessed with facts, dates and precise detail. My dad was always careful to get his facts right, but his main interest was in people.

Dad knew all about the people who built Jesmond, and the wealthy industrialists who originally occupied its grand houses. And as we were growing up, he seemed to know most of the people who were living in Jesmond in the 60s and 70s! Dad loved talking to people, and talking about people, and that was how he was constantly expanding his vast archive of information. That formidable database, combined with a wonderfully wry, working-class sense of humour, made him one of the most entertaining local historians you could hope to meet. When we brought school friends home Dad would always ask them where they lived, and instantly produce nuggets of information about the house or street they lived in, or the people who'd lived there in the past (or the people who were living there at the time, for that matter). Somehow he had everything cross-referenced in his head, so he could instantly link the history of different houses, people or places, and enliven any conversation with an interesting fact. But his greatest gift was his ability to communicate all that knowledge in such a spontaneous way, his stories always punctuated with laughter. Dad could always find something to laugh about.

Born in Heaton and brought up in Shieldfield, Dad's interest in Jesmond was triggered in the 1930s when he started work as a milkman, making horse-drawn deliveries up Osborne Road. It became his ambition to live in Jesmond, and after national service in Germany he attended the Anglican Youth Club at St George's church (the church was gifted to the parish by the wealthy shipbuilder Charles Mitchell, of course), where he met my mother Kay. He officially became a Jesmond resident in 1956 when they began their married life together in Sunbury Avenue. For as long as I can remember every journey in Dad's car was made to a soundtrack of stories about the places

Chris Donald

Jimmy Donald outside 16 Lily Crescent.

we were passing, and of course the people who'd lived there. The names of the houses, their owners, the builders, even the land owners, were drilled into us. Our house in Lily Crescent was full of history. As well as collecting maps, books, pictures and photographs, Dad accumulated real pieces of Jesmond history. The door bell from St George's vicarage, demolished in the 60s; a giant urn salvaged from the gable end of the

Lily Crescent in around 1910.

house which stood where Tesco's is today; an ancient stone marking the boundary of one land owner's estate. We had some interesting garden ornaments in Lily Crescent.

There was enough information inside Dad's head to fill several volumes on the history of Jesmond and the people who have populated it over the years, but his priority was always talking and listening, not writing. Sadly, illness robbed of him of his ability to communicate in his latter years, and it also prevented him adding to the small number of books he had produced, and of which he was rightly proud. But I'm delighted that **Jesmond from mines to mansions** is now being published in his memory, and it's nice to think that through his knowledge, his enthusiasm and his ability to inform and entertain so many people over the years, Dad has managed to earn his own little place in the history of Jesmond.

Chris Donald, 2010

The leafy suburb of Jesmond

Jesmond today is a busy suburb to the north east of Newcastle city centre, but at the end of the 18th century the township of Jesmond was predominantly agricultural, made up of fields and meadows, with scattered coalpits and a small population of less than 200.

For most of its recorded history, Jesmond encompassed just over a square mile, or approximately 700 acres (about three-quarters of the size of the neighbouring Town Moor), with boundaries at the Craghall Burn to the north, the Ouseburn to the east, Sandyford Road to the south and the Town Moor to the west.

In earlier days Jesmond may have taken in a larger area. The first recorded name, Gesemue (early 13th century), means 'mouth of the Ouse', and at that time the township probably did reach down to the river Tyne, where it is thought a salmon fishery existed. Later, from the 14th century, references to 'Jesmound', 'Jesemond', or 'Gesemonte' occur and this may reflect the movement of the township's southern boundary about a mile and a half upstream to roughly where it is today. The clerics at St Mary's Chapel may then have referred to it as either the 'mount of the stream' or Jesus Mount, because of its raised position above the Moor Crook Letch stream. The modern spelling of Jesmond dates from the 17th century.

Historical background

A few isolated prehistoric artefacts have been found in Jesmond including a stone axe head and a few stone built graves (containing bones and pottery) but, so far, no trace of Roman occupation has been discovered.

Northumberland and Durham were excluded from the Domesday Book of 1086, and the earliest recorded date connected with Jesmond is found in the early 1100s, when King Henry I granted the township to one Nicholas Grenville, probably of French descent, of whom little else is known, in exchange for the service of three knights. The Grenvilles, as Lords of Jesmond, almost certainly built St Mary's Chapel and the first known Manor House. Granville Road is a present day reminder of Nicholas Grenville.

From the 12th century there emerges a line of Lords of the Manor of Jesmond as families intermarried, died out, or even swapped land in various deals. Some of the better-known include Adam of Jesmond, a 13th century royalist sheriff of the rebellious county of Northumberland, as well as Keeper of the royal castle at Newcastle. The remains of his fortified house may be seen today in Heaton Park. Robert Bruce the Elder was the 13th century grandfather of Robert I King of Scots who had acquired land in Jesmond through his marriage to Christiana, the widow of Adam of Jesmond. William Cavendish was a Royalist general during the 17th century Civil War, who had inherited land in Jesmond from his mother, Catherine Ogle, a Northumbrian heiress. As one of the richest men in England, and related to the Devonshire family, he became Duke of Newcastle as a reward for his enormous financial support for the king. William Bentinck was the 18th century second Duke of Portland, who married a Cavendish heiress.

Farming

During the middle ages, most of Jesmond would have been divided into cropland, pasture and common land. The cropland consisted of three huge fields, which were rotated on an annual basis. One field would be autumn-sown with wheat and rye. Another field would be planted with spring crops, of barley, oats, peas or beans. The third field would be left fallow. Pasture (known as the leazes) for the growing of hay and then as a grazing area for cattle after the harvest lay in the area covered today by Mitchell Avenue and Towers Avenue. Common land for the general grazing of cattle and the provision of turf for fuel, heather for thatching and bedding, as well as wood for general use, lay to the north of the pasture where the Matthew Bank area is now, plus Jesmond Dene as far south as Jesmond Dene Terrace. Jesmond's common land, when compared with other townships, was small relative to its arable fields probably because the Town Moor would have provided further uncultivated ground.

Each of the three large fields, known in 1631 as the North Field, the Middle Field, and the East Field, was subdivided into half-acre strips or rigs, separated from each other by a narrow strip of unploughed turf. Farmers were each allocated around 48 of the strips (usually 220 yards by 11 yards) over the three fields so that everyone had a fair and equal share of both good and poor land. Later, to make farming more profitable, these numerous and isolated unenclosed rigs of land were consolidated into larger units known as 'flats' and ultimately into fenced fields.

People working on the land and in local industries, at this time, would have lived in thatched cottages, each with its small enclosure or garden opening on to the village green, which probably lay close to St Mary's Chapel, Jesmond Manor House, and Stote's Hall in the area now covered approximately by lower Reid Park Road and Grosvenor Avenue.

By the late 18th century the land in Jesmond had been fully enclosed, either by hedges or fences, to create in the region of 80 named fields (see the map opposite) and farmers, instead of living around the village green, had moved elsewhere in the township to settle in purpose-built farms. Around 1800 there were five such farms: Matthew Bank, covered today by Sturdee Gardens; North Jesmond, which became North Jesmond House, near the junction of Jesmond Dene Road and Matthew Bank; Moor Edge, immediately south of Lyndhurst Gardens railway bridge between Highbury and the Metro line; Friday Farm, near the junction of Haldane Terrace and Otterburn Terrace; Minories, close to the Punchbowl Hotel on Jesmond Road.

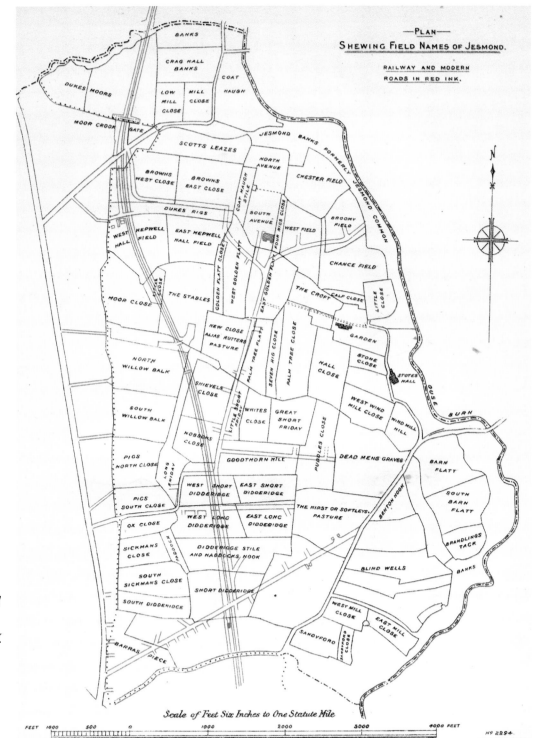

This map of Jesmond field names is reproduced from F.W. Dendy's Account of Jesmond, 1904.

Coalmining

Coalmining was carried out as an industry in Jesmond over at least 250 years. The last public notice concerning coalmining in the area appeared in a local newspaper in 1845 when it was stated that coalmining operations were then only being carried out near Jesmond Cemetery.

It is impossible to locate the Jesmond coal pits precisely, but around 30 sites are mentioned in general correspondence. Some pits took the name of the fields where they were situated (such as Puddles Close, Palm Tree Close, and Chance Field) while others such as Mayflower, Resolution and Margaret Pits cannot be identified. However, with at least 80 fields in Jesmond it seems likely that many of them must have contained pits or mines at one time. The reason for the large number of small pits is that in the 17th and 18th centuries, before more advanced methods of digging, draining and ventilation evolved, it was more practical to sink fresh pits at short distances from each other than to work underground.

In the earliest days coal was dug from the sides of the Ouseburn Valley by means of shallow workings. An early map of south-east Northumberland (c1600) marks five pits in Jesmond, but does not name them or give their exact position.

In 1625 a reference exists to at least one Jesmond mine having reached a depth of 22 fathoms (132 feet) at which time the method of lifting and lowering coal baskets and miners was most likely to have been by whin gin. This apparatus consisted of a drum fixed over the mineshaft, activated by a horse yoked to a horizontal bar which in turn was connected by cog wheels to the drum. The horse plodded steadily around the circular track causing the drum to revolve and so lift, by means of a rope, wound around the drum, the basket of coal, maybe 3 or 4 cwt (150kg-200 kg) or a miner.

By around 1670 horse-driven chain pumps were in general use to drain mines of water and usually consisted of buckets attached to an endless chain. At this time the raising of water from a depth of 40 fathoms (240 ft) was considered a great achievement. Apparently it was the water from Jesmond Colliery (centred on Fern Avenue) that in 1815 caused the flooding of the nearby Heaton Main Colliery and the death of 75 men and boys.

By 1725 there were several collieries in

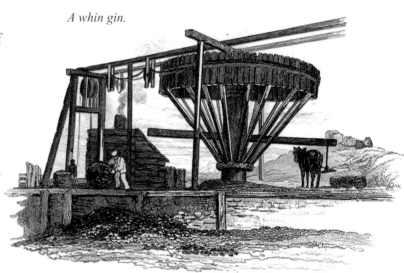

A whin gin.

Jesmond and upwards of 700 carts employed in transporting coal, with the water being drawn from the colliery by means of horse engines.

Jesmond Colliery is marked as 'old pit', with a house, on the mid-19th century map on page 12. It was owned by Sir Thomas Burdon and situated by the Mill Burn approximately where Fern Avenue meets Gowan Terrace

This detail from a hand-coloured view engraved around 1832 looks south over a rural Jesmond. The Ouseburn meanders south towards the Tyne long before its wooded valley was made into a garden and park by Lord Armstrong. The chimneys of Busy Cottage ironworks, just about where Pets Corner is today, smoke in the middle distance. Jesmond village is to the right of the picture, on the high ground, hidden amongst the trees, and beneath the ground there are extensive mine workings. Jesmond Dene Terrace has not yet been built, but Stote's Hall is on the hillside to the west above the valley.

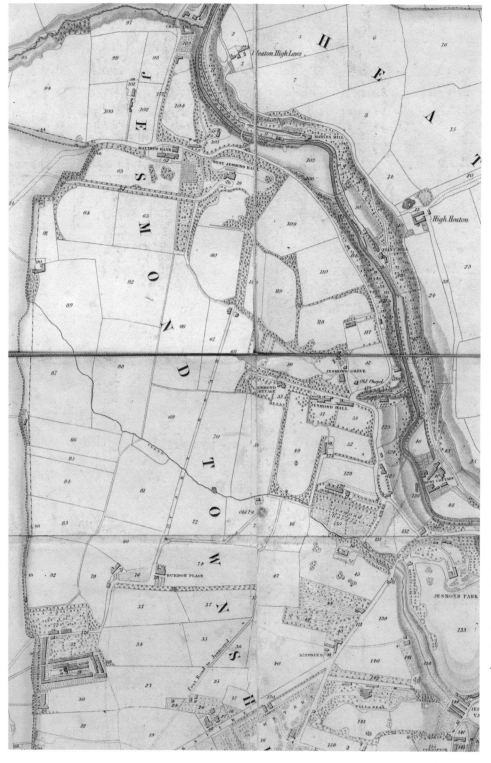

Thomas Oliver's map, published in 1844 (reduced in scale here), shows Jesmond before the railways arrived, but after coalmining had come to an end.

The fields are all enclosed, and there are a few cottages east of the Manor House or Hall. Some large Victorian mansions have appeared, as well as the first of the new cemeteries and some of the new roads.

There are a few residential developments such as those at Brandling Village, Jesmond Place and Jesmond Dene Terrace.

You can see the Mill Burn in the middle of the map, flowing in a south-east direction all the way from the Town Moor to the Ouseburn.

today. The former Co-op grocery building (now an antiques village) stands on or near the site. From here a wagonway to carry coal followed a route along present day Holly Avenue, Osborne Road, Haldane Terrace and Clayton Road to coal staiths and a depot for landsale coal at the south-west corner of Abbotsford Terrace. Cottages were also situated near the staiths and Brandling Village, built in the 1820s, lay close by. The earliest recorded date for Jesmond Colliery is 1631. In 1658 an individual named James Arthur is reported as having been drowned at the pit. Then, apart from the colliery being damaged by strikers in 1831, no other information is available.

A second pit (the only other mine to be marked on the early 19th century map referred to earlier) was still being worked in 1823, again on land belonging to Sir Thomas Burdon at a place near the open grass-covered area in front of St George's Church. A wagonway ran from this pit down what is now Osborne Road to meet the other wagonway from Jesmond Colliery. The depth of this mine in 1823 was 42 fathoms (252 ft) but no other information, or its name, has been found.

There were at least two compensation claims for damage to private buildings caused by mining activities. In 1745 William Coulson, who built the last Jesmond Manor House in 1720, was able to claim the cost of repairing cracks to his home. In 1823 compensation was awarded to the owners of Jesmond Grove, Jesmond Manor House and Jesmond Cottage for damage caused by subsidence.

A few other references to mining in Jesmond survive. In 1826 Sir Thomas Burdon sank a colliery close to Villa Real near Jesmond Cemetery. In 1828 an old shaft near the Minories was re-opened after being out of use for 84 years; and in 1831 vandalism occurred at a pit being sunk in a field near the Great North Road, when the rope which hung down the pit was 'burnt in two'.

Footpaths and roads

Five recognised footpaths are recorded in the township at the beginning of the 19th century and these are the ancestors of some of today's streets. Church Walk led from Barras Bridge north-east to Jesmond Village and St Mary's Chapel along the course of the present Fernwood Road and Manor House Road. Another footpath led from Sandyford Bridge (Lambert's Leap) via what is now Hutton Terrace to join the Church Walk near Jesmond Road. Friday Fields Lane, also called the Lovers' Walk, branched east from the Great North Road near to the coal staiths to follow present day Burdon Terrace, then headed north along Tankerville Terrace (past Friday Farm), St George's Terrace, and North Jesmond Avenue to Jesmond Dene Road. Part of this route survives as a diversionary footpath between Towers Avenue and Jesmond Dene Road. An east-west footpath crossed over Friday Fields Lane approximately where Acorn Road joins St George's Terrace, to connect the Great North Road (via a track following present day Forsyth Road) with Jesmond village via Acorn Road. Again, part of the footpath remains, the result of another diversion, to pass to the north side of Jesmond Cottage. A footpath from Jesmond Vale crossed Jesmond Road and headed towards Stote's Hall and on to Jesmond village.

The only proper roads in Jesmond around 1800 followed its boundaries – the Great North Road to the west and Sandyford Lane to the south. Jesmond Road (at first named Cemetery Road) was not planned until the 1830s. Jesmond Dene Road was not a through road at this point – a short section existed to the north between the Great North Road and the Moor Crook Letch (Osborne Road junction) and a similar brief length of road in the south between Benton Bridge and Jesmond village. In the mid-19th century Jesmond Dene Road was created by the connection of these earlier routes. At first this new road formed an awkward loop to the south west of St Mary's Chapel, because of the need to cross the Moor Crook Letch and pass the entrance gate to James Losh's mansion at Jesmond Grove (see map on page 78). In 1871 this dangerous bend near the chapel was eliminated by building an embankment over the Moor Crook Letch to the south-east of the chapel (with two pedestrian tunnels beneath) to rejoin the old road a short distance to the north. The old colliery wagonways were converted into roads in Victorian times.

Streams

Culverted many years ago, four streams flow beneath Jesmond into the nearby Ouseburn.

The Crag Hall Burn formed the boundary between Jesmond and Gosforth. It rises on the Town Moor and flows along the north side of the Duke's Moor across the former Great North Road (indicated by a dip in the road) along the north side of Lodore Road, through Crag Hall Dene (infilled with soil from the early 20th century railway extensions in central Newcastle), then enters the Ouseburn immediately north of Crag Hall.

The Moor Crook Letch (letch means boggy ground) rises near the junction of Osborne Road and Jesmond Dene Road and passes in front of St George's Church and then through the former Jesmond Grove estate (Reid Park Road area) close by St Mary's Well and Chapel and then enters the Ouseburn immediately north of Jesmond Dene Terrace.

The Mill Burn rises near the junction of Grandstand Road and Kenton Road, flows past Forsyth Road railway bridge and then beneath Mistletoe Road, across Osborne Road (where there is a dip) down Queens Road and across Manor House Road (where there is another dip), then across Jesmond Road at the dip at the south end of Shortridge Terrace and then enters the Ouseburn near Jesmond Vale Bridge, where it once powered a watermill.

The Sandyford Burn rises on the Town Moor near the foot of Cow Hill. Flowing through Exhibition and Brandling Parks it then follows the line of the east Central Motorway to Sandyford Road under Lambert's Leap (the former Sandyford Bridge), to enter the now culverted Ouseburn beneath the present landfill site, forming one of Newcastle's largest refuse tips for much of the 20th century.

Residential development

The first significant sale of land for residential development took place in 1805, and this event marked the beginning of change in the nature of the township. During a period of just over a century, Jesmond was transformed from a rural township, with some industrial activity, into a residential suburb. The population rose dramatically from 275 in 1801 to 15,364 by 1901 and to over 20,000 by 1911.

In around 1800, residents would have been familiar with over 80 fields and closes with several footpaths but very few roads. There were at least five farms, two windmills, and four watermills (in the Ouseburn Valley). Jesmond Colliery and other pits, Busy Cottage Ironworks in the Ouseburn Valley and a few local sandstone quarries provided industrial employment. There would have been several cottages for agricultural and industrial workers, situated by the village green near the Manor House, at the colliery staiths and at Crag Hall. There was also a hamlet of cottages known as the Minories near Sandyford Bridge. There were two public houses – the Grapes and the Apple Tree Inn. The notable buildings were Jesmond Manor House, Stote's Hall, St Mary's Chapel (ruined) and the associated well. St Andrew's Church in central Newcastle was Jesmond's parish church where baptisms, marriages and funerals took place though many of the leading inhabitants chose St Nicholas churchyard at South Gosforth as their burial place.

Land began to be sold off gradually to property developers during the first half of the 19th century, and this resulted in the

Georgian housing in Brandling Place South, built around 1820. The photograph is dated c1910..

construction of several large villas and mansions for the growing number of wealthy individuals. North Jesmond House and West Jesmond House were built for Sir Thomas Burdon. South Jesmond House was built for William Armstrong (father of William George). Jesmond Park was built for Armorer Donkin. Jesmond Grove was built for James Losh. St Mary's Mount was built for Edward Moises. Jesmond Dean was built for William George Armstrong.

As the century progressed isolated groups of terraced houses began to be built for the middle classes: Burdon Place, Carlton Terrace, Collingwood Terrace, Fenham Terrace, Jesmond Villas, Jesmond Place (later Gardens), Victoria Place (later Square) and Warwick Place. Brandling Village was constructed for the increasing number of artisans attracted to the area. Although by 1851 the population had risen to 2,089, Jesmond remained essentially a rural suburb of Newcastle into which it had been incorporated in 1835 along with Byker, Heaton,

Tyneside Flats, pictured around 1910 in Forsyth Road, looking east, towards the railway bridge.

Elswick and Westgate.

It was the coming of the railway in 1864, which ran from north to south through the middle of Jesmond that acted as a catalyst to its future development. This section of the railway, managed by the Blyth and Tyne Company, was, unusually, designed for passenger rather than goods traffic and so able to compete for customers with the nearby and popular Newcastle to North Shields railway. They were prepared to carry Third Class passengers at a time when many other railways did not, and also ran a half-hourly service on bank holidays between Newcastle and Tynemouth. The Blyth and Tyne also built a 'spacious and commodious' platform near Moor Edge Farm for horse racing fans attending the Town Moor meetings. This platform (now removed) was about 300 yards north of the present West Jesmond Station which opened in 1900.

It was during the second half of the 19th century that Jesmond became built-up and it was almost complete by the outbreak of the First World War, except for parts of estates belonging to more recent landowners. Meanwhile, Jesmond's population had rocketed from 2,230 in 1861 to over 20,000 some 50 years later. Most dwellings were two-storey terraced houses of variable size, with a sprinkling of substantial villas.

From the mid-1860s stage one of the housing explosion centred on the Jesmond Road area, on either side of the railway station, and took around a decade to complete. The streets involved included Windsor Crescent, Place and Terrace, as well as the following terraces: Akenside, Benton (look out for the original street names on the corner of Sandyford Road and Portland Terrace), Hutton, Osborne, Percy and Portland.

The next stage involved the large central area on either side of Osborne Road from around 1875 and building went on over around 20 years. The final phase of building began in 1895 following the sale of land by the Duke of Portland (and others) to the Forsyth brothers as potential builders, and the construction of the West Jesmond Estate. The Forsyth brothers introduced the Tyneside Flat to Jesmond.

Because a large proportion of this new housing was designed as flats for 'working men' many of Jesmond's residents became extremely angry and threatened an exodus to nearby Benton. The prospect of a 'Board' school arriving in the near future merely caused further anxiety as seen in this letter in the popular magazine *Northern Gossip*, and the cartoon on page 18, dated May, 1897.

Another problem arose a few years later because of the

JESMOND AND ITS FLATS.

A Jesmond correspondent writes:—Dear "Gossip,"—You would smile a cynical smile if you could but note the strangely altered circumstances in Jesmond. There is now a perfect rush of working men to the flats erected in West Jesmond, and facing Gosforth. This is bad enough in all conscience, but when you consider that Tankerville Road and other swell streets are made the thoroughfares between the flats and the public-house in Brandling, you may know our unhappy position. Children with their jugs, pots and cans on weekdays, and the workingman himself, a little toddles in one hand and a jug in the other, on Sundays, are common pictures. Quarterly notices are rife on all hands. The glory has departed from Jesmond.

The only pots in Jesmond
(And of these there still are lots),
That we only wish to sanction
Are the "Pots" who hate the pots.

THE EXPECTED EXODUS FROM JESMOND TO BENTON.

[A Deputation from Jesmond has approached the Council against the introduction of a Grammar School and Workmen's Flats.]

Duke of Portland having included a 'non-intoxicating liquor' clause in his earlier sale of land contract. An application in 1906 to build an hotel at the junction of Lonsdale Terrace and Lyndhurst Avenue on a vacant site near the recently opened West Jesmond Station was refused. Supporters of the proposed hotel claimed to be of the 'superior working class' and did not see why they should have to walk around a mile to the nearest pub. One of these pubs was the North Terrace on Claremont Road and it was said that a beaten track to it, known as the 'Beer Track' led across the Town Moor. A cinema and shops were later to occupy the vacant site until, in 1951, the Lonsdale pub replaced the shops. The cinema site at present awaits redevelopment.

It is now around a century since Jesmond became built-up and, except for the increase in road traffic, someone returning from around 1910 would not notice that much of a change. Most of the infrastructure remains intact except for the demolition needed for the construction of the East Central Motorway in the 1970s, and the alterations at the east end of Jesmond Road when the Cradlewell Bypass was constructed in the 1990s. Of course the cobbled streets have been resurfaced.

Many of Jesmond's mansions have been converted into apartments or into commercial properties. Some have been demolished and rebuilt. A huge influx of students from the local universities during the last few decades has resulted in many of the terraced houses being converted to bed-sits, so consequently the character of some streets has changed, for the time being at least. Finally, to meet the demand for entertainment and leisure, several of the substantial terraced houses on Osborne Road have been transformed into hotels, nightclubs and restaurants.

A view along Sunbury Avenue towards St George's Terrace, around 1910. The pillar box remains in position on the corner with Lonsdale Terrace and is one of the few similar Victorian post boxes in Jesmond.

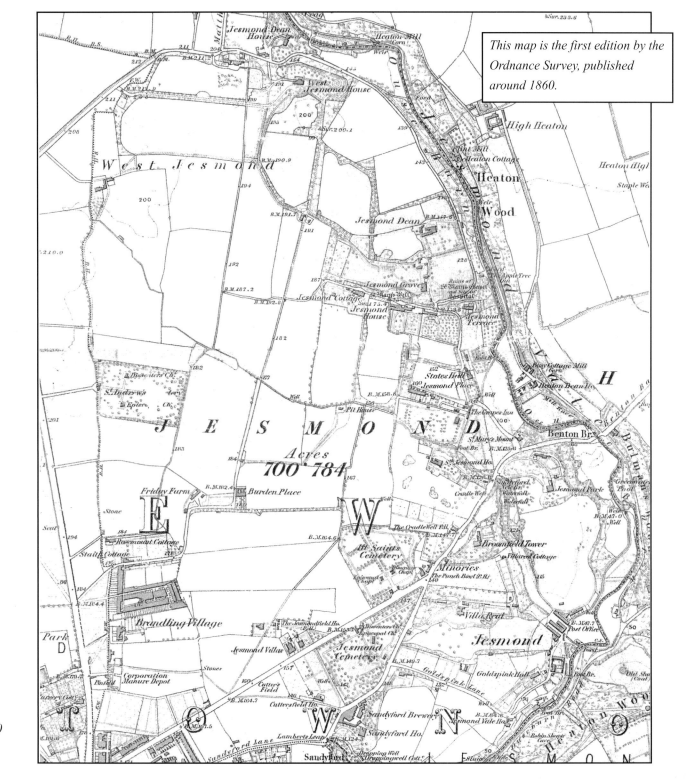

This map is the first edition by the Ordnance Survey, published around 1860.

20

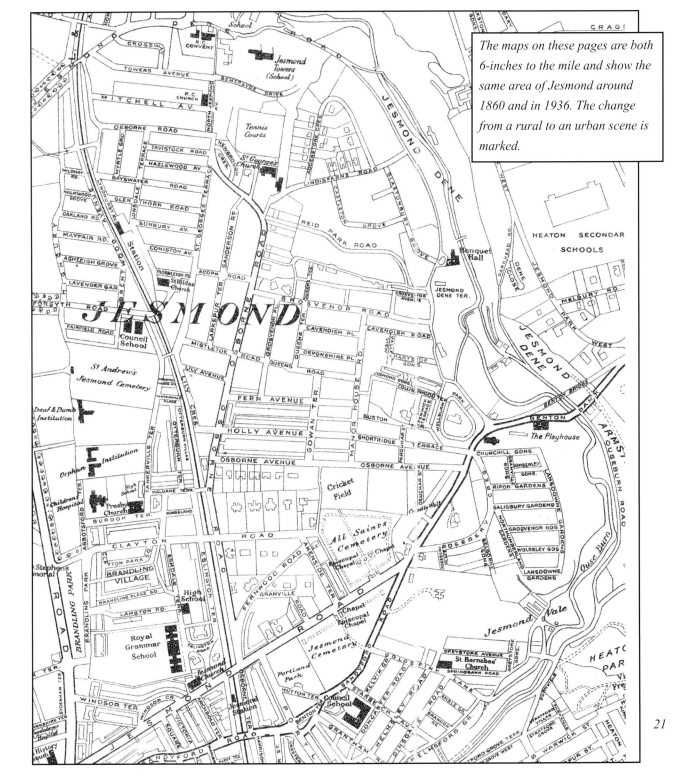

The maps on these pages are both 6-inches to the mile and show the same area of Jesmond around 1860 and in 1936. The change from a rural to an urban scene is marked.

Exploring Jesmond

The following pages are set out in the form of five linked circular walks, though the walks could certainly be carried out from your armchair.

We have used a 1936 map (slightly enlarged from 6-inches to the mile), opposite, to guide you through each walk, along with Oliver's 1844 survey of the same area, as a comparison.

Jesmond, 1844

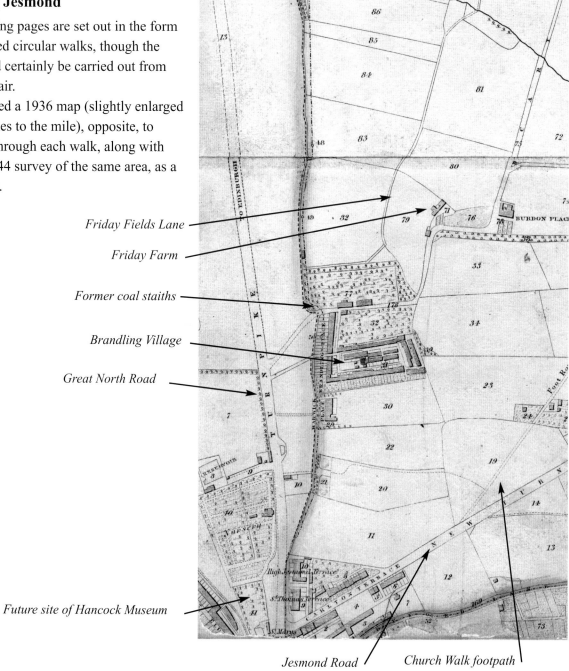

Friday Fields Lane

Friday Farm

Former coal staiths

Brandling Village

Great North Road

Future site of Hancock Museum

Jesmond Road

Church Walk footpath

Walk 1: From Jesmond Station

1. Jesmond Station (now The Carriage pub)

2. Jesmond Road

3. Jesmond Parish Church

4. Royal Grammar School

5. Lifton House

6. Newcastle Preparatory School

7. Central High School

8. Brandling Village

9. Brandling Park

10. The W.D. Stephens Memorial Fountain

11. Fleming Memorial Hospital (now Business Centre)

12. Orphan Institution (Princess Mary Court)

13. Deaf and Dumb Institution (Northern Counties School and College); (*now follow path to Great North Road*)

14. St Andrew's Cemetery (*now exit to Tankerville Terrace*)

15. West Jesmond School

16. Church High School

17. United Reformed Church

18. Jesmond Synagogue, Eskdale Terrace

19. Methodist Church, Clayton Road

20. Eslington Terrace

21. Private hospital, Eslington Terrace

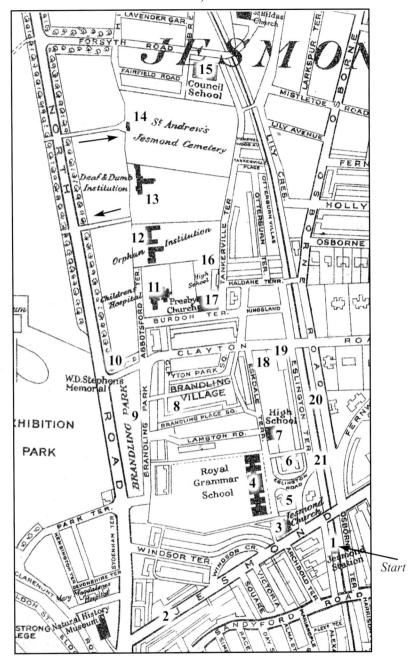

Jesmond, 1936

1. Jesmond Station, c1910

Jesmond Station opened in 1864 when the Blyth and Tyne Railway extended their branch line into Newcastle with a terminus at New Bridge Street. At this time Jesmond was still largely rural with fields and meadows surrounding the station, although some recently built terraced housing and Sandyford Road lay to the south.

The Blyth and Tyne Railway encouraged passenger travel by offering Third Class travel several years before their competitors which was to bring prosperity to local coastal resorts as well as increasing attendance at popular attractions such as horse racing, theatrical promotions and agricultural shows. A 'Race Week Special' operated between New Bridge Street and Moor Edge, for the Town Moor racecourse, at a return fare of 3d. The Moor Edge platform was situated a short distance north of the present West Jesmond Metro Station.

The line was electrified in 1904 in response to serious competition from local electric tram-cars to become the first suburban electric rail system in the country outside London.

This photograph is dated to approximately 1910 and at that time the coaches would have had a livery of red (below) and cream (above), and a clerestory roof, together with a combined route and destination board above the driver's cab. This train was heading south towards Manors North.

In 1980 the station was replaced by a new underground station for the Metro Rapid Transport System a little way to the north across Jesmond Road. The old station buildings that remain now operate as a pub and restaurant. In the distance, the lofty spire belonged to Jesmond Methodist (Wesleyan) Church, now demolished.

2. Jesmond Road, 1920s

This photograph looks east along Jesmond Road from near the Great North Road. The substantial three-storey brick houses, with basements, on the right (or south side) formed an elegant terrace of ten homes built about 1840. A similar terrace on the opposite side of the road (partially hidden by trees) was designed by John Dobson around 1838, and was known as Carlton Terrace.

Jesmond Road was for several years called Cemetery Road simply because it led to Jesmond Old Cemetery, designed by John Dobson and opened in 1836. Carlton Terrace was the earliest housing on this thoroughfare.

The terraced houses on the right were then extended along the road up to 12 years later. In fact the point of architectural change can be seen and is where the bay windows appear at ground floor level and also where the 'blind' third floor windows of the earlier 1840 development are no longer a feature,

In the late 1960s, Jesmond Road, by then a very busy commuter route, was bisected by the Central Motorway East and this western sector became a quiet backwater and cul-de-sac. Carlton Terrace is presently occupied as part of Newcastle University while on the opposite side of the road the premises are either commercial or residential.

The last trams on this route had been phased out by 1949 and replaced by trolley buses although the Osborne Road 'trolleys' had appeared as early as 1938.

3. Jesmond Parish Church, 1860s

This first parish church in the new and rapidly growing suburb of Jesmond, 'Midst green fields and meadows', opened in 1861. Built in the Gothic style to the design of John Dobson it could seat 1,340 people, about one-third of whom were seated in the galleries. The planned for spire was never built because of insufficient funds. Sometimes referred to as Clayton Memorial Church, it was a memorial to the ever popular Richard Clayton who died suddenly in 1856 after serving many years as an Evangelical chaplain at St Thomas's Church, Barras Bridge. When it became known he was to be replaced at St Thomas's by a 'High Church' vicar, a furious group of worshippers decided to break away and plan a new church – Jesmond Parish. Since the new church was not dedicated to any saint, the opponents of the breakaway group nicknamed it St Spite. Richard Clayton was the younger brother of John Clayton, the former Newcastle Town Clerk, who was involved in the town's redevelopment in the 1830s and after whom Clayton Street was named.

Jesmond Parish Church soon after it opened.

This photograph is dated 1937. Today the church's surroundings have changed dramatically as it sits uncomfortably above slip roads to and from the adjacent motorway. There is now only pedestrian access from Jesmond Road. The new underground Jesmond Metro station is nearby.

This view of the Royal Grammar School taken from the tower of Jesmond Parish Church in around 1910 shows in the distance, from left to right, the houses of Brandling Park, Lambton Road, Brandling Village, and further off the Fleming Memorial Hospital, the Northern Counties Orphanage, and the Northern Counties Deaf and Dumb Institution. Beyond is the Town Moor.

4. The Royal Grammar School, c1906

The Royal Grammar School moved to this spacious site at Brandling Fields, Jesmond, in 1906 from their previous school at Rye Hill which had never been satisfactory. Rye Hill had been in the wrong catchment area to attract sufficient pupils, the school was running into debt and it lacked ample playgrounds. Brandling Fields, the school's sixth home since its foundation in the 16th century had been a ten acre recreation field before its transformation into palatial two-storey buildings together with playing fields and sufficient space for future expansion. Initially the school was built to accommodate about 500 boys at a total cost, for land and buildings of at least £60,000.

There is a long cherished school tradition when the pupils receive an annual visit from the newly elected Lord Mayor of Newcastle and are then granted holiday for that day. This custom dates from around 1600 when the school moved into the former Hospital of St Mary the Virgin at Westgate, only to find the Corporation was occupying part of the premises as an election room for the mayor and other officials. Westgate remained the school's second home for about 240 years.

Alongside an entrance in Eskdale Terrace are two octagonal sandstone columns rescued from the 12th Century former hospital at its demolition in 1844.

GRAMMAR SCHOOL, NEWCASTLE. 5267. G.K.N/C.

5. Lifton House, 1890 and 1968

At noon on 22nd September 1890, over 7,000 boilermakers and shipbuilders from the North East Region assembled at Newcastle's Central Station ready to march to Jesmond and celebrate the opening of their Society's new permanent headquarters at Lifton House next to Jesmond Parish Church. A day's holiday had been granted by employers. Large crowds lined the route to witness the marching bands colourful banners and the symbolic emblems carried by the men. These emblems included miniature ships, sections of boilers as well as model forges, some of which contained real fires and figures of men whose limbs moved by the pulling of strings.

Following the ceremonial opening by Sir B.C. Browne, chairman of Hawthorn Leslie & Co Ltd, the gathering moved to a nearby football field (now covered by the Royal Grammar School) where several speeches were made from the grandstand. Essentially a square structure of rough freestone, the new building contained spacious offices and committee rooms plus a residence for the secretary. The cost amounted to approximately

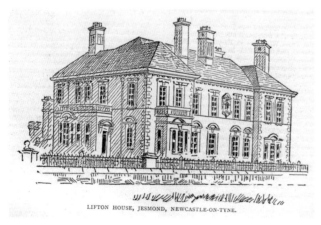

LIFTON HOUSE, JESMOND, NEWCASTLE-ON-TYNE.

£8,000. The drawing on the left appeared in the *Monthly Chronicle*, Autumn 1890.

Several alterations and extensions have since taken place and today the building is occupied by the National Probation Service for England and Wales.

The origin of the name Lifton is unknown but may have a connection with a village of that name in Devon.

6. Newcastle Preparatory School, corner of Eskdale Terrace and Eslington Road, 1971

Newcastle Preparatory School was founded in 1885 by local businessmen in two adjoining but separate three-storey houses. At first there were only 11 boys, some of them boarders. According to an early school prospectus the school rooms were 'large and lofty, thoroughly ventilated, well lighted, equipped with modern educational appliances and with sanitary facilities receiving special attention.' An excellent sports field of two or more acres was close by with an open-air gymnasium at one end (now enclosed)

As pupil numbers increased adjoining properties were added and today the school teaches around 260 girls and boys in houses on Eslington Road.

The photograph shows Eskdale Tower in the centre. Old boys of the school include Cardinal Basil Hume (1923-1999) who spent time here in the early 1930s. He became Archbishop of Westminster and leader of Britain's Roman Catholics.

7. Central Newcastle High School for Girls, Eskdale Terrace, c1900

In 1876 Gateshead High School for Girls opened, with space for 28 pupils, at Prospect Cottage Bensham. A group of prominent local families, in particular that of the Quaker Robert Spence Watson, had been the driving force behind it. It was immediately a popular school and increasing pupil numbers made it necessary to move to a purpose-built school at Windmill Hills Gateshead (now demolished) in 1880. Towards the end of the 19th century a feeder school opened in Newcastle to attract more pupils from north of the Tyne to Gateshead. The school became successful but now with many more pupils from Newcastle than Gateshead new premises were opened at Eskdale Terrace in 1900 to become the Central Newcastle High School for Girls. Meanwhile the school at Windmill Hills continued to cater for Gateshead-based girls until 1907 when it closed and merged with the school at Eskdale Terrace.

The school belongs to the Girls Public Day School Trust and currently has a total of nearly 1000 pupils spanning the age range from three to 18. Pupils are split over several sites including Seniors at Eskdale Terrace, Juniors at the former Nazareth House (Sandyford) and Infants at West Avenue, Gosforth.

8. Brandling Village, c1910

The Manor of Jesmond had been a farming and coal mining area from an early period but in 1821 the sale of land for the creation of what eventually became Brandling Village, probably marked the beginning of what would become the first residential suburb in Jesmond. By the late 1820s 'about one hundred convenient freehold houses and cottages' had been built close to the Great North Road to provide accommodation for the growing number of artisans in the area. It is interesting to note that by 1833 there were three pubs in this small area, the Coal Waggon, the Brandling Arms, and the Collingwood Arms (two of which survive, rebuilt, today). Sir Thomas Burdon's coal staiths lay at the north side of the village with the colliery about half a mile away to the north east. The village name is said to commemorate Charles John Brandling, the former MP for Newcastle, land owner and coal magnate. The photograph clearly shows the chimney of the Brandling Laundry and wash room which operated for about 90 years in a building that once had been a Wesleyan Methodist Chapel. Most of the houses were condemned and demolished in the 1930s and a carpark now occupies most of the space.

9. Brandling Park, 1897

Brandling Park near Brandling Village opened in 1880. Newcastle's mayor (Richard Cail) declared the park 'open and free to the public' and spoke of how much better it was to walk in the park rather than indulge in 'gross amusements'. Three years later it is said, Newcastle 'had more open spaces reserved for public recreation than any other large town in the Kingdom'.

The small five acre park was created from part of the Town Moor, transformed by drainage from rough open pasture into manicured grassy plots with several meandering paths. A bowling green occupied the north end (and is still there) and a croquet lawn lay at the south end with a small lake (and islet) and water fountain in between. Carriageway widening of the Great North Road in the late 1960s considerably reduced the area of the park. In the background of this 1897 photograph are some of the substantial terrace houses known as Brandling Park. There is another view of Brandling Park on the title page of this book.

10. The W.D. Stephens Memorial Fountain, corner of Clayton Road and North Road, 1908

This memorial fountain was dedicated to the public life of William Davies Stephens (1827-1901) and unveiled by Thomas Burt MP in May 1908. This photograph, taken at the ceremony, demonstrates the popularity of the occasion. Abbotsford Terrace lies beyond the crowds.

Born at Alston, the son of a lead mining agent, Stephens arrived on Tyneside to work for a few years in the commercial department of a chemical manufacturer before changing direction to become a shipbuilder and ship owner. Stephens sold his business to the Tyne Tees Shipping Company, where he eventually became a director.

As a staunch Wesleyan Methodist, in retirement Stephens became a social reformer and a supporter of the temperance movement. He also became involved in local politics as a councillor and later rose to become sheriff, mayor and alderman. During this period there were very few charities that escaped his support and for many years he was also a governor of the Infirmary. Perhaps his major charitable achievement was in being the driving force in the establishment of the Town Moor Annual Temperance Festival, the hoppings, after the racecourse moved from the Moor to Gosforth Park in 1881.

11. The Fleming Memorial Hospital for Sick Children, Moor Edge, c1888

Opened at Moor Edge in 1888 by Lord Armstrong, this children's hospital was the gift of John Fleming, a Newcastle based solicitor, in memory of his late wife Mary. There were beds for 60, as well as convalescent facilities, and the cost was nearly £23,000. This three acre site had previously been the home of Newcastle Cricket Club. The photograph shows the hospital soon after opening.

An earlier children's hospital was founded at Hanover Square in 1863 by a group of public-spirited medical men to accommodate children from the nearby but run-down Infirmary. It relied heavily on gifts in kind such as 'a jar of dripping, a parcel of rhubarb and green peas' from a Mrs Middleton. John Fleming's generous offer eventually solved the problem of serious overcrowding.

The Fleming continued to depend on public support until the establishment of the National Health Service. Methods of raising cash included cot endowments, the collection of silver paper and concerts staged by local dancing schools at which, on one occasion, Alicia Markova performed.

In 1987 the Fleming closed and the staff and children were transferred to the Royal Victoria Infirmary. Today a Business Development Centre occupies the buildings of the former hospital.

12. Northern Counties Orphanage (later Princess Mary Maternity Hospital), Moor Edge, 1880s

The Northern Counties Orphanage began in rented rooms at Clayton Street West in 1864 and moved to these new and extensive buildings at Moor Edge less than ten years later thanks to the generosity of two prominent local families.

The girls' orphanage (in the photo) was paid for by Mrs Catherine Abbot in memory of her husband who had managed the Park Iron Works at Gateshead. 'Abbot Memorial' is inscribed in stone within the central pediment. The boys' orphanage (off the photograph and to the right) was financed by the son of the former Newcastle town clerk, Ralph Park Philipson, in memory of his mother who had taken a deep interest in the work of the orphanage and became known as the 'Philipson Memorial Orphan Asylum'.

Both orphanages evacuated to Cumbria during the Second World War and almost immediately the buildings were occupied by the Princess Mary Maternity Hospital who moved here from Jubilee Road in central Newcastle. The hospital transferred to the Royal Victoria Infirmary in 1993.

The buildings have now been converted into private apartments and are known as 'Princess Mary Court'.

13. Northern Counties Deaf and Dumb Institution, Moor Edge, c1920

The Northern Counties Institution for the Deaf and Dumb opened at Moor Edge in 1861 to accommodate 60 residential pupils. Founded at Wellington Court (now demolished) off Pilgrim Street in 1838 it catered for deaf and dumb as well as blind children from Northumberland, Durham, Cumberland and Westmorland. In 1849 the deaf and dumb children moved to a large house at Charlotte Square while the blind children re-located to the Royal Victoria Asylum for the Industrious Blind on Northumberland Street.

At Moor Edge, several extensions and alterations have taken place since 1861 largely funded by donations, subscriptions and legacies to enable larger numbers to be accommodated. HRH Diana Princess of Wales visited the school in 1988 to celebrate the 150th anniversary of its foundation.

Now known as the Northern Counties School and College, it caters for all types of disabled children and is one of the most up to date schools of its kind in Britain with excellent facilities including swimming, hydrotherapy pools, a light stimulation room and outdoor play areas.

14. St Andrew's Cemetery, 2003

St Andrew's municipal cemetery opened in 1858 on this ten-acre site at Moor Edge. It replaced St Andrew's churchyard in central Newcastle following the closure by Act of Parliament of all urban parish churchyards. Municipal cemeteries had the major advantage over churchyards of being much larger in size. They also catered for all religions.

At that time the surrounding area was completely rural, the nearby railway had not yet arrived and the Great North Road provided the only approach to the new cemetery. There have been just over 43,000 burials to the present time. Familiar personalities interred here include: Ralph Hedley the artist and wood engraver, Sir G.B. Hunter the shipbuilder and Eileen Blair, the wife of the novelist George Orwell. Dr William Errington and Marie Hume, parents of Basil Hume, are buried here too. You will also find the graves of Dr Thomas Emerson Headlam, physician and Whig politician, and John Burghersh Forbes, hero of Balaclava.

The photograph looks east from the cemetery buildings near the Great North Road. To the left of the carriageway is the Nonconformist section and to the right is the consecrated section for Church of England burials.

15. West Jesmond School, Tankerville Terrace, 1964

As Jesmond's population continued to expand during the 1890s it desperately needed a local school. A two acre site was acquired in West Jesmond bounded by Forsyth Road, the railway, St Andrew's Cemetery, and Brentwood Avenue. A temporary 'tin' school opened in 1901 to cater for 300 infants while permanent school buildings were under construction.

The permanent infants' school opened in 1902 (as in this photograph) facing what is now Tankerville Terrace, for 300 pupils, then in 1905 a permanent junior and senior school opened in separate buildings facing Forsyth Road to accommodate 1,100 children. These three buildings were designed by Newcastle architect, Charles S. Errington. The school buildings were in a cul-de-sac until Tankerville Terrace was extended in 1912 to join Brentwood Avenue by way of an awkward bend.

According to the memories of early pupils each classroom held 50 to 60 children sitting at double desks usually with hands behind backs or even on heads so as to allow lungs to expand! Talking in class was forbidden and corporal punishment a normal part of life. Each teacher was provided with a leather strap but apparently to have your name entered in the Head Mistress's Black Book was considered to be much more of a disgrace.

The outside toilets, adjoining the cemetery wall, were bleak and an ordeal for some as queuing was usually necessary. Occasionally the school closed at times of epidemics, and coats were needed in cold weather.

A new school opened on this site in 2008 following the demolition of the earlier buildings.

16. Newcastle upon Tyne Church High School, Tankerville Terrace, 1890s

Miss Helen Gladstone, daughter of the Liberal Prime Minister, opened this new high school for girls in 1890 at Tankerville Terrace. It was Jesmond's first purpose-built school premises and accommodated about 300 girls. The impressive red brick building was designed by the well known local architects Oliver and Leeson and included a science laboratory, dining hall, kitchens and a large gymnasium.

Newcastle High School was founded in 1885, in four terrace houses at 54-60 Jesmond Road, by the Church Schools Company. An existing ladies' seminary and boarding school at this address formed the nucleus of the new school. Most of this property survives and is now used for commercial purposes.

In 1925 the school was re-named Newcastle upon Tyne Church High School.

At one time boarders were accommodated at The Grove, near St Mary's Chapel, and part of the grounds used as playing fields. The school at Tankerville Terrace was enlarged in the 1930s and a new Junior School added in 1974 largely funded by the sale of the playing fields at The Grove for residential housing.

17. Jesmond United Reformed Church, Burdon Terrace, c1912

Originally Presbyterian, this church opened in 1888 at the corner of Burdon Terrace and Tankerville Terrace. It seats about 850 people. Newcastle's first Presbyterian church was at Garth Heads (1743) then Sallyport (1762), next Carliol Street (1823), and Barras Bridge (1873) where they remained for about 15 years.

W.L. Newcombe designed the new buildings in the Early English style to include a large lecture hall with classrooms and accommodation for a caretaker. A significant feature of the church is the substantial square tower rising to a height of 90ft (27m). The total cost of land and buildings amounted to £11,000.

Mr William Sutton, a church founder and original Elder, as well as a draper and outfitter, had the honour of becoming Newcastle's first Presbyterian Mayor in 1891. A stained glass window to his and Mrs Sutton's memory is at the south end of the church.

In 1972 the Presbyterian Church of England merged with the Congregational Church in England and Wales to form the United Reformed Church (URC).

The Lecture Hall can be seen to the left of the church and to its right is the high roof of the Church High School in Tankerville Terrace.

Living at No. 20 Burdon Terrace (nearly opposite the church) for 30 years was Thomas Burt (1837-1922), the first working miner to become an MP. He was the Northumberland Miners' Leader for many years, and was General Secretary of the Northumberland Miners Association for 48 years. A plaque identifies the house.

18. Jesmond Synagogue, Eskdale Terrace, 1915

The problem of travelling on foot from Jesmond to the Leazes Park Road Synagogue in Newcastle, particularly for the elderly and the young of Jesmond's Jewish community, was solved when a synagogue on Eskdale Terrace was opened in 1915. At around the same time, an additional burial ground was acquired in a section of Byker and Heaton cemetery at Benton Road.

Founder members of the new synagogue included several prominent local businessmen including Moses Jackson (Jackson the Tailors), Joseph Cohen (Woodhouse's retail furniture store) and Gabriel Woolf (the first Jewish councillor in Newcastle and the Synagogue's President for many years).

Because of population expansion a synagogue opened in the 1980s at Graham Park Road in Gosforth, to eventually absorb the synagogues at Eskdale Terrace and Lansdowne Terrace. Eskdale Terrace Synagogue closed in 1986.

The building is now occupied by the nearby Central Newcastle High School as their Art Department and is appropriately named Russell House after Newcastle's first Jewish Lord Mayor (Alderman Dr H. Russell) and his wife, Newcastle's first Jewish JP (Alderman Mrs Theresa Science-Russell). Mrs Russell also served as Lord Mayor.

19. Jesmond Methodist (Wesleyan) Church, Clayton Road, c1912

Jesmond Wesleyan Church opened in 1883 as an overflow for the crowded Brunswick Methodist Chapel in Newcastle and also to cope with the rapidly expanding suburb of Jesmond. A temporary Iron Chapel was in use from 1877 while the necessary funds were being raised. Several well known Newcastle businessmen were involved as trustees and guarantors including E.M. Bainbridge, T.H. Bainbridge, G.B. Bainbridge, J.J. Fenwick, W.D. Stephens and W.H. Stephenson.

Mr J.J. Lish was appointed architect. The design in modified Gothic was to provide seating for 850 in the church, 350 in a lecture hall and 180 in a large vestry and also to include premises for a caretaker. A lofty clock tower and spire completed the buildings at a total contract price of nearly £7,000.

Nearly a century after its opening, the church was demolished in 1981 because of falling attendances and economic pressures. Today, apartments managed by the Methodist Homes for the Aged, and known as Pilgrim's Court, cover the site.

This view of the church was taken from the railway bridge. Eslington Terrace branches off to the left.

20. Eslington Terrace, 1910

Residents in 1910, when the terrace was around 30 years old, included department store owners Henry A. Murton and Arthur Emerson Bainbridge, and Thomas Oliver junior, architect. Eslington Terrace beyond Clayton Road was not completed until 1915. Most of the houses have now been converted into flats.

21. This double-fronted three-storey dwelling, Eslington House, was a private hospital and nursing home when the photo was taken in 1910. The building is situated at the south end of Eslington Terrace almost adjoining Eslington Road.

Built around 1880 as a home for Robert Deuchar the local brewer, it was later a preparatory feeder school for the Gateshead High School for Girls (see page 32).

After functioning as a private hospital and nursing home over about 25 years, the house became a ladies' hostel for a further decade. The building was converted into flats in around 1933.

Eslington House, 1910

Jesmond, 1844

Thomas Oliver's 1844 map shows us a rural Jesmond of fields and farms.

Crag Hall Burn

Crag Hall

Matthew Bank Farm

Black Dene

North Jesmond House

Avenue to West Jesmond Hall

Jesmond Dene Road

Farm track, still there today

Moor Edge Farm

Friday Fields Lane

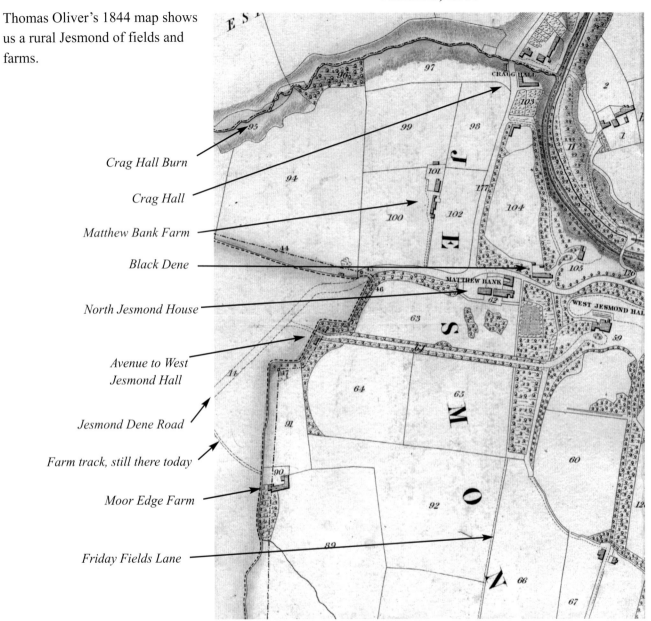

The numbers on the fields refer to an index naming the land owner together with the acreage of fields, buildings or plantations.

Jesmond, 1936

Walk 2: From West Jesmond Station

1. West Jesmond Station
2. Jesmond Picture House
3. Osborne Road (upper bend)
4. West Lodge and Towers Avenue
5. Matthew Bank Farm
6. Crag Hall
7. Real Tennis Court
8. Jesmond Dene House
9. North Lodge
10. North Jesmond House (*now
    go down the footpath to
    Towers Avenue*)
11. Jesmond Towers
12. The Holy Name RC church
13. Mitchell Avenue
14. Northumberland Club
15. South Lodge
16. Tram terminus
17. Osborne Road (lower bend)
18. Tavistock Road

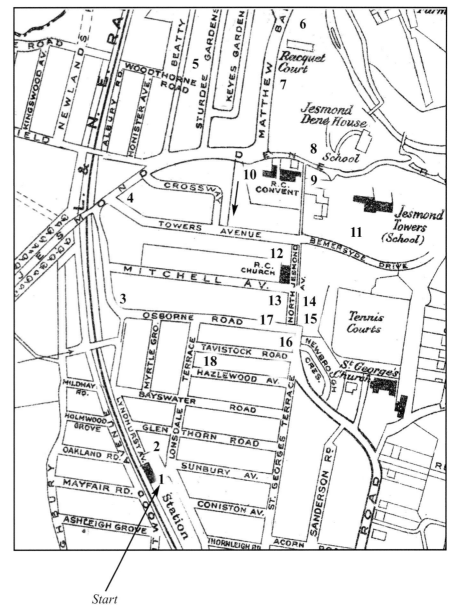

Start

1. West Jesmond Station, 1910

West Jesmond station opened on 1 December 1900 specifically to serve the surrounding neighbourhood being built by the Forsyth brothers. The railway service from Newcastle to the coast had already been operational for over 35 years.

The new station included various waiting rooms on both sides of the track, each with their own 'patent fireplace'. The gentlemen's first class room is a 'snug little apartment with table and hair covered seated chairs and an oil cloth on the floor'. The ladies' first class room 'is similar and has lavatory accommodation in a room adjoining. There is also a general room for ladies where they may wait in seclusion.' Another general room presumably for men, 'is lined out with glazed bricks and has seats running right round.'

There were also separate rooms for staff. Outside the station was 'a cosy little dwelling', for the station master and his family. Alongside the track were sidings for coal and goods together with a weigh house to deal with the expected increase in rail traffic. At this time the ordinary single fare for passengers to New Bridge Street was one penny and to Tynemouth, eightpence (a shilling return).

The new residential area had been nick-named Klondyke because of its general inaccessibility and also because the district frequently resembled a quagmire as homes were built before roads. Originally there were plans to actually name the station 'Klondyke', but they came to nothing, which was probably just as well!

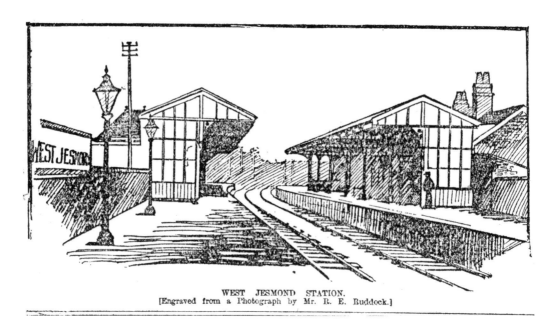

WEST JESMOND STATION.
[Engraved from a Photograph by Mr. R. E. Ruddock.]

This photograph was taken about 1910 and shows an electric train heading north to Benton.

The drawing opposite is from the Newcastle Journal for 1 December 1900, opening day. The station was 'remarkably handsome, and is fitted up with the latest improvements, rendering it in every way adapted to meet the considerable traffic that is expected.' A 'substantial subway' connected (and still connects) both sides of the station.

Today's Metro Station is spartan compared with just over 100 years ago with no rooms, staff or sidings. The former railway sidings and goods yard are now covered by the Lonsdale Court flats and the British Legion Club.

2. Jesmond Picture House, 1965

Jesmond Picture House opened in 1921 opposite West Jesmond Station. It seated about 1000 people and cost nearly £35,000 to build. Regarded as 'absolutely fireproof' and spacious, it also made watching the screen from the front stalls more comfortable by having a floor with a reverse slope. The advertisement is from November, 1950.

The cinema was never wholly successful, but it survived the post-war television boom owing to a number of factors including the large number of students living in the area and its convenient proximity to the railway together with a reasonable pricing policy. Later, for several years, bingo and films shared the building until bingo sessions ceased in 1977.

By 1984 the 'Jesmond' was one of only three commercial cinemas remaining in Newcastle compared with 41 in 1939. The cinema closed several years ago and was demolished in 2009. Today the site awaits development.

3. Osborne Road, 1910

This photograph of the upper part of Osborne Road about 1910 highlights one of the two abrupt curves necessary to avoid the boundary of the late Charles Mitchell's estate. The photograph was taken from near the junction with Lyndhurst Gardens and Jesmond Dene Road is in the distance. Most of the visible houses, completed around 1907, are now occupied by students and because the road is so busy with constant traffic the area has become unsuitable for young children. On the opposite side of the road are larger semi-detached houses, some with their construction dates displayed on terracotta plaques.

OSBORNE ROAD, NEWCASTLE. 1611.

4. Jesmond Towers West Lodge, c1920 and Towers Avenue, c1932

This rural photograph of the tree-lined driveway that originally connected West Jesmond House (later Jesmond Towers) with the outside world at Jesmond Dene Road was taken about 1932. The carriageway became Towers Avenue around 1935-1937.

West Lodge, right, built by Charles Mitchell in the 1870s and photographed here in 1920, stood at the junction of his carriageway and Jesmond Dene Road. Sadly it fell victim at a later date to housing developments.

5. Matthew Bank, 1890s and 1941

Matthew Bank farm, the last surviving farm in Jesmond, stood around where Sturdee Gardens is today, until replaced by semi-detached houses from around 1932.

The three acres of land along the south bank of the Crag Hall Burn (Jesmond's northern boundary) is named Matthew's Bank on early 19th century maps. Thomas Atkinson of Crag Hall owned the land but it remains a mystery as to who Matthew was.

Substantial improvements were made to Crag Hall Lane (now Matthew Bank) around 1828 by making it more direct and reducing the gradient. A hundred years later, during the preparation for the new housing development, this became one of the areas in Newcastle to benefit from the re-use of stone following the demolition of the old gaol in Carliol Square. Beatty Avenue, Sturdee Gardens and Keyes Gardens were named after high profile British Admirals who had visited the home of Sir Andrew Noble at nearby Jesmond Dene House. In December 1941 five persons were killed when a World War II bomb devastated a few houses near the foot of Matthew Bank.

Matthew Bank Farm, North Jesmond, 1891.

ncjMedia

6. Crag Hall, 1973

Crag Hall was once a short row of stone-built miners' cottages, said to date from 1788, on the south bank of the Crag Hall Burn. They were converted into a house for Dr Thomas E. Headlam in 1814 before he moved up-market to Black Dene on Jesmond Dene Road. The Crag Hall Burn once formed the boundary between Jesmond and South Gosforth and in 1893-94 the upper part of the burn was culverted and infilled with spoil from the railway widening programme in central Newcastle. In 1844 two Bronze Age graves were uncovered in the grounds of Crag Hall by a gardener and some of the contents are on view at the Great North Museum. The house has been a care home for the elderly since 1982.

7. Real Tennis Court, 2010 and Jesmond Dene Nurseries, 1940s, Matthew Bank

The Real (or Royal) Tennis court on Matthew Bank, at the far end of the extensive gardens of Sir Andrew Noble's Jesmond Dene House, opened in 1894 with an exhibition match between Charles Saunders the world professional champion and Sir Edward Grey MP, an amateur champion related to the former Northumbrian Prime Minister Charles Earl Grey. At that time it was one of just seven such courts in Britain.

Noble, an active tennis player who continued to play into his eighties, engaged F.W. Rich, the talented local architect, to design the bright red brick building, together with an attached two-storey dwelling to accommodate a full-time professional player. The specialised interior layout of the building was planned by Joseph Bickley, considered to be the most famous of tennis court architects.

During the First World War the court was used for making airship gasbags and water ballast bags, and throughout the Second World War the building served as a storage depot for the Highways Department.

In recent times the court has flourished as a Real Tennis Club.

The remainder of Noble's garden between his home and the court is Newcastle City Council's nursery garden for plants, which moved here in the 1930s.

The greenhouses above, just north of the Real Tennis court, were photographed in the 1940s. Crag Hall is just visible, far right. Note also the empty space (upper left) on Matthew Bank, the result of bomb damage in 1941.

8. Jesmond Dene House, Jesmond Dene Road, 1964

The first house built on this site was Black Dene, designed in 1822 by John Dobson for Dr Thomas E. Headlam, a Newcastle physician and politician. In 1862 Sir Andrew Noble, a director at Lord Armstrong's Elswick Works, moved here from Heaton Cottage in Jesmond Dene and immediately had the house enlarged by Norman Shaw (Cragside's architect). Noble renamed it Jesmond Dene House.

In 1896, as Elswick Works flourished and clients and guests needed accommodation, Frank Rich, a talented local architect, was engaged to completely rebuild the property into a 39-roomed mansion. Many distinguished visitors have stayed here including the British admirals Beatty, Sturdee and Keyes, De Havilland (the aircraft designer), Rudyard Kipling and Baden Powell.

After the death of Lady Noble in 1930 (aged 100), Newcastle Corporation purchased the 13-acre estate and extended Jesmond Dene to Dene Bridge near Castle Farm.

Since then, the mansion has had several occupants. Before World War II it housed the Newcastle College and High School for Girls, and then during the war it became Newcastle's Civil Defence Headquarters. After the war, it served as a hostel and social club for the newly founded Ministry of National Insurance at Longbenton, followed by a period as offices for the National Assistance Board. Then for over 40 years it functioned as a special school for children with learning difficulties. Today it operates as a hotel and restaurant.

9. Jesmond Towers, North Lodge, 1920

Probably built about the same time (1870s) as the West Lodge, to serve as a tradesmen's entrance to Jesmond Towers, this rather attractive building is on Jesmond Dene Road nearly opposite Jesmond Dene House. The gateways were blocked with a wall to prevent access to La Sagesse school in the 1970s.

Between this lodge and the top of Matthew Bank is an inscribed stone placed low down in the roadside wall marked 'WS 1820'. It may have been a boundary stone connected with the former farm and nine acre field known as Scott's Leazes.

NORTH LODGE, JESMOND TOWERS, NEWCASTLE. 1554.

10. North Jesmond House, 1964

This substantial house, the back of which can be seen from the top of Matthew Bank, was built in 1821 for Sir Thomas Burdon. It later became the home of shipbuilder Henry Frederick Swan a younger brother of Charles Sheriton Swan (of Swan Hunter) and brother-in-law of Charles Mitchell, shipbuilder. The grounds of North Jesmond House adjoined those of Charles Mitchell's property at Jesmond Towers. Henry Swan's major contribution to shipbuilding was the development of oil tankers, and while living at this address he designed the first tanker to carry bulk petroleum across the Atlantic.

In 1912, the nuns of La Sagesse School took over the house. A new building for boarders (later the Junior School) opened in 1923 and five years later a chapel was added. The school expanded into neighbouring Jesmond Towers in 1948 which became the Senior School. The school closed in 2008.

11. Jesmond Towers, 1920

The original West Jesmond House was built by architect John Dobson in 1817 for Sir Thomas Burdon, brother-in-law of Lord Eldon, landowner, brewer and former Mayor of Newcastle. In 1827 Dobson enlarged the building for Richard the only surviving son of Sir Thomas. Richard had already married the daughter and heiress of Sir James Sanderson, Lord Mayor of London and MP, to become Richard Burdon-Sanderson in accordance with the terms of his father-in-law's will.

In 1869 Charles Mitchell, the important Tyneside shipbuilder, bought the property, made substantial additions and re-named it Jesmond Towers. Mitchell's great passion was art and because his son, Charles William became a talented artist a fine studio and a large picture gallery were added to the home (see page 60). An insurance inventory of 1883, valued the house at £14,000 and then his pictures, sculptures and jewellery at an extra £14,267. By contrast, the servants' effects were valued at just £150. There is a ghost story attached to the house. Charles Mitchell's sister-in-law, Emily committed suicide by throwing herself from the tower and her ghost is said to haunt the building as a pink lady.

Following the death of Charles Mitchell junior's wife, the estate became a private school in 1932 for boys and girls from the age of five. At that time the fees, including books and games amounted to £3 8s a quarter. Later, a boys' preparatory school occupied the property, and in 1948 La Sagesse Convent took it over as their Senior School until the school closed in 2008. The building and grounds await development.

Charles William Mitchell's picture gallery at Jesmond Towers in 1910. The painter Francis Bacon was related to the Mitchell family through a great aunt and, as a child, he visited Jesmond Towers around 1915 where the paintings provided his first introduction to fine art. The gallery became the gymnasium and assembly hall for La Sagesse Convent school.

12. Church of the Holy Name (Roman Catholic), 1964

The Roman Catholic parish of the Holy Name at Jesmond was founded in 1901 in a terrace house on Manor House Road in which one of the rooms served as a chapel. Two years later a temporary iron church opened on St George's Terrace (now the site of Jesmond Pool) where it functioned for 26 years.

By 1928 the Building Fund for a permanent church had grown to a reasonable sum so a prominent site at the corner of Mitchell Avenue and North Jesmond Avenue was acquired. The foundation stone was laid later that year.

The Holy Name, designed by Roger Fenwicke (of Dunn Hansom and Fenwicke), opened in 1929. It seats 400 and there is a presbytery for at least two priests. It cost £15,238 to build. Meanwhile the earlier iron church was sold and re-erected at Murton Colliery village in County Durham where it survived for another 34 years.

A new Parish Centre opened near the church in 1972 and at this time Lady Hume (mother of Cardinal Basil Hume) lived in the parish close to the church.

13. Nos. 4-12 Mitchell Avenue, 1920

These four large semi-detached houses and a villa are at the east end of Mitchell Avenue near to North Jesmond Avenue and St George's Cricket Ground (hidden by trees). These five homes were completed by 1913 with space left at either side for later additions. Semi-villa No. 14 was built in 1925 to the left and four years later the Church of the Holy Name opened at the end of the road.

This avenue of varied and spacious dwellings for some of Tyneside's leading businessmen was completed about 1938 on part of the estate belonging to the late Charles Mitchell, the well known local shipbuilder and philanthropist.

Mitchell Avenue can also be seen in the 1926 photograph opposite, top left. Towers Avenue would be built where the avenue of trees leads towards Jesmond Towers, top right.

MITCHELL AVENUE, NEWCASTLE 2560

14. Northumberland Tennis Club, 1926

This eight-acre site north of St George's Church, opened as St George's Cricket Club around 1890 on land owned by Charles Mitchell. Charles William Mitchell, his son, a great advocate of open air sports and already president of the club then presented the ground to the Cricket Club a few years after his father's death in 1895.

By the early 1920s lawn tennis was becoming very popular and a permanent home was sought for

Towers Avenue *Mitchell Avenue* *North Jesmond House* *Real Tennis court* *Matthew Bank Farm* *Jesmond Towers* *Adderston Crescent*

Northumberland's inter-county matches. So, in May 1926, at a cost of around £26,000, all subscribed by local members, this new and spacious home for the Northumberland Lawn Tennis Association was opened by the future King George VI. The ground was considered 'second to none' outside of London and consisted of 25 courts (mostly turf, some shale), a covered stand and dressing rooms. Local tennis clubs (Brandling, Jesmond, Lindisfarne and Osborne) were encouraged to lease courts. Improvements have taken place over the years and in the mid-1990s an indoor centre was added, sunk partially below ground to blend in with its surroundings.

This informative photograph was published in *Newcastle Journal*, May 29, 1926, the day after the opening, and shows how rural Jesmond was at that time.

15. Jesmond Towers, South Lodge, 1920

The Jesmond Towers estate eventually had three entrances each with its own gates and a lodge. The South Lodge, as photographed in 1920, remains at the junction of Osborne Road and North Jesmond Avenue. It was built later than the other two lodges because of the need to connect the estate with the growing importance of Osborne Road. The date '1883' and initials 'C M' can be seen in the decorative plaster work above the bay window. On the left hand gate pillar, one of the scallop designs is upside down and said to be the result of a disgruntled stone mason.

16. Osborne Road Tram terminus, c1910

This photograph was taken near Osborne Road's junction with St George's Terrace. Tram No. 7 from the Central Station, via Grainger Street and Monument or via the Arcade, is at the terminus and about to return to the station. At the tram terminus, Osborne Road swings sharp left between the low level tramways shelter and the large house behind. Beyond the tram is North Jesmond Avenue where the houses were not completed until 1937. To the right of the tram can be seen the roof and chimney pots of Jesmond Towers South Lodge among the trees.

North Jesmond Avenue lies over Friday Fields Lane which once connected Friday Fields Farm (Haldane Terrace area) in a direct line to South Gosforth via what is today Tankerville Terrace, St George's Terrace, North Jesmond Avenue, Jesmond Dene Road and Matthew Bank. Following the arrival of Charles Mitchell at Jesmond Towers a subway for the public using Friday Fields Lane was created at a point where it met his carriage drive (now Towers Avenue). After Jesmond Towers became La Sagesse School, the subway was closed and the Friday Fields Lane footpath to Jesmond Dene Road replaced by an alternative path at the west side of the school's property. This later path remains in use today.

17. Osborne Road, 1910

This photograph looks west along upper Osborne Road in about 1910 from near its junction with North Jesmond Avenue. Osborne Road has two awkward corners in this area because of the need to avoid crossing the estate belonging to the late Charles Mitchell. The first of these corners is at the North Jesmond Avenue junction and the second is in the distance, where the houses appear to block the road.

The houses in the photograph are still largely as they were a century ago but this once tranquil suburban street is now a very busy thoroughfare with constant traffic. Osborne Road is now classified as the B1600. A cyclist today attempting a carefree manoeuvre in the middle of the road would be at severe risk. The terraced flats on the left, were built around 1903 while the semi-detached houses on the right side of the road date from about five years later.

18. Tavistock Road, 1910

This photograph looks east along Tavistock Road towards Osborne Road. The trees at the far end would become part of the Newbrough Crescent residential development of the 1930s. The 87 houses in Tavistock Road were largely completed 1902-1904 and consist mainly of Tyneside Flats together with some self-contained two-storey homes. The house on the far left is To Let.

For 27 years from 1938 yellow trolley buses used Tavistock Road and Lonsdale Terrace as a turning loop for the Central Station to Osborne Road service.

TAVISTOCK ROAD, NEWCASTLE. 1894.

Jesmond, 1844

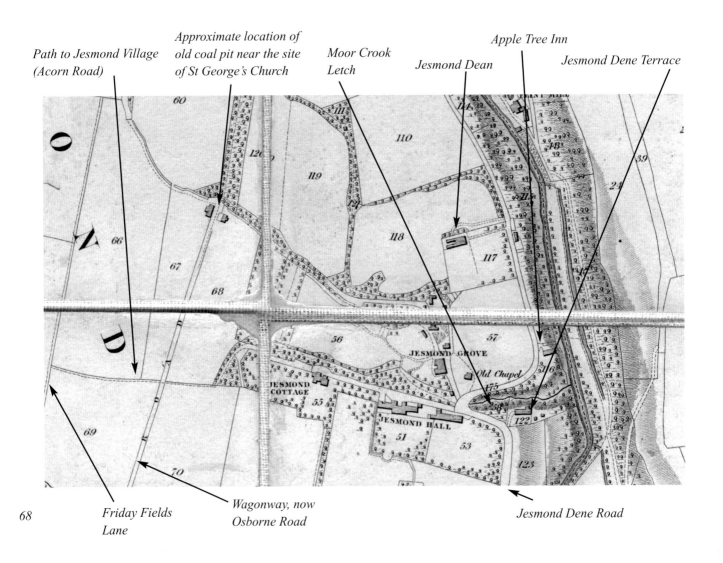

Path to Jesmond Village
(Acorn Road)

Approximate location of
old coal pit near the site
of St George's Church

Moor Crook
Letch

Jesmond Dean

Apple Tree Inn

Jesmond Dene Terrace

Friday Fields
Lane

Wagonway, now
Osborne Road

Jesmond Dene Road

Walk 3: from Jesmond Pool, Glenthorn Road

1. Jesmond Pool
2. Osborne Road
3. St George's Church
4. Jesmond Lawn Tennis Club
5. Adderstone Crescent
6. Jesmond Dean
7. The Banqueting Hall

8. St Mary's Chapel
9. Jesmond Grove
10. Apple Tree Inn
11. Jesmond Manor House
12. St Mary's Well
13. Jesmond Cottage
14. Grosvenor Villas

15. Osborne Road
16. Acorn Road
17. St George's Terrace
18. Methodist Church, Library
19. St Hilda's Church

Jesmond, 1936

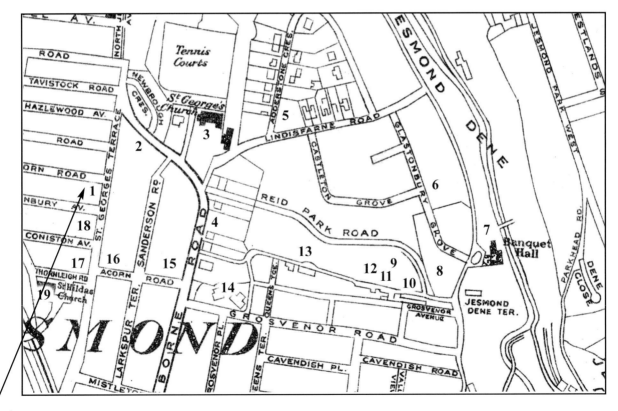

Start

1. Jesmond Pool, Glenthorn Road, 1968

Jesmond Pool opened in 1938 on a site which had been occupied by the temporary Roman Catholic Church of the Holy Name. The church re-opened in a new building on Mitchell Avenue in 1929.

Apart from the usual dressing rooms, cubicles and lockers the new building boasted Art Deco decoration and was designed for 'purposes other than swimming' during the winter. Indoor bowling began in 1948 and continued every year from October to April until the Eldon Square Recreation Centre opened in the 1970s. Jesmond residents had regularly campaigned during this time for swimming throughout the year, but to no avail.

In 1991 the pool closed owing to Local Government spending cuts despite 'Save our Pool' demonstrations and a 'sit-in'. One year later it reopened as a Company Limited by Guarantee with Charitable Objects thanks to sponsorship, grants, merchandising and the endeavour of many volunteers. At this time it was unique for a municipal pool to have been taken over by local residents.

Following restoration, refurbishment and redecoration the pool continues to be a well-supported community sports and leisure centre.

Right: the tin church of the Holy Name, St George's Terrace, between Glenthorn Road and Bayswater Road, around 1903.

Below: St George's Terrace with the tin church in the distance, around 1910. Sunbury Avenue is on the corner, left.

2. Nos. 129-139 Osborne Road, c1910

This impressive row of six red brick houses, originally private dwellings, on Osborne Road between Sanderson Road (left foreground) and St George's Terrace, just opposite St George's Church, was completed around 1901. No. 131 served for over ten years as the Northern Counties Training College of Cookery and Domestic Science. No. 133 operated as the regional Division of the National Council of the YMCA for at least 20 years while its neighbour No. 135 was a private school for a short period.

3. St George's Church, c1888

By the early 1880s there was an urgent need to provide a parish church for the rapidly growing suburb of north Jesmond. At that time the Rev. Somerset Pennefather was vicar at the nearby Jesmond Parish Church on Jesmond Road and he and his family were frequent visitors to Charles Mitchell, wealthy local resident and shipbuilder, at Jesmond Towers. The families may well have discussed the possibility of a new church and parish for Jesmond and Charles Mitchell offered to pay for a complete new church and vicarage to be built on part of his estate. First Mitchell bought a temporary iron church which had been used at St George's in Cullercoats but it soon proved too small so a much grander church was planned on the condition that Mitchell could have the church designed according to his wishes. The foundation stone was laid in January 1887. The Diocese must have been extremely grateful. Pennefather became St George's first incumbent.

Thomas Ralph Spence, a young architect, perhaps better known as a local artist, was appointed to prepare plans with the added comments from Mitchell that 'it is not what it costs but what is best'. Eventually the attractive and spacious buildings cost the huge sum of over £30,000 which is not surprising considering that only the very best quality materials were used and it included everything, 'even down to the hymn books'.

The architectural style was largely influenced by Mitchell's European travels and the distinctive and lofty bell tower, 254ft high (78m) excluding the cross, is said to be based on the campanile of St Mark's in Venice. The church, which seats 700 persons, was consecrated on 16 October, 1888.

To the left of the church is the vicarage (later demolished and rebuilt nearby) and to the right is the parish hall, paid for by parishioners. Osborne Road runs in front of these buildings and the open land, between this road and the church, which remains today was also purchased by parishioners. Jesmond Towers, home of Charles Mitchell is just visible in the distance between the church and vicarage.

4. **Jesmond Lawn Tennis Club, Osborne Road**

Jesmond Lawn Tennis Club celebrated its centenary in 1983 and remains the oldest club in Newcastle to survive in its original form as well as being one of the oldest in the world.

Founded in 1883 at Fern Avenue, the club (whose logo is a fern leaf) moved seven years later to Osborne Road where they had five grass courts and a pavilion. At this time there was an active membership of 102 and the annual subscription cost £1 10s for men and one guinea for ladies. The land was rented from Mr Burdon-Sanderson at £30 a year until the ground was purchased outright in 1920. In 1973 two of the original five courts were converted to red shale and then several years later both courts nearest to Osborne Road were sold for a residential development now known as The Lawns. A private footpath runs from Osborne Road to the courts alongside the Lawns but general access is now via Reid Park Close to the rear. Interestingly the club's name and foundation date are inscribed on an arch over a lockable iron gate at the Osborne Road entrance. At present there are three 'all weather' courts together with floodlighting and a pavilion.

One of the club's major highlights must have been in 1902 when one of its members, 24-year-old Muriel Evelyn Robb, won the ladies' singles championship at Wimbledon. In preceding years she had also triumphed in the 'mixed doubles' and three times in the 'doubles' as well as being the first lady to win all ladies' singles titles of the four home countries. A native of Newcastle and related to the well known Robb family of Hexham, she lived at various addresses in Jesmond until she died after a lengthy illness at the early age of 28. She was buried in the family vault at Jesmond Old Cemetery and at her funeral it is reported that the wreaths were so numerous that two lorries were required to convey them to the cemetery.

These photographs show Muriel Robb at Wimbledon in 1902.

From 'Lawn Tennis' by A.W. Myers

5. Adderstone Crescent, c1910

These newly-built mansions, on Lord Armstrong's land, are Hunstanworth, Oaklea and Holm Lodge to the left and Ruthven, and Chesters Close to the right. Occupants of these substantial homes before World War I included shipowners, solicitors, a shipbuilder and a tea merchant. Another resident was the future Sir Angus Watson, a food manufacturer and philanthropist, chiefly known for Skipper Sardines. Some of these properties, with new names, are now apartments, and of course the cobbles have gone. The connection with Adderstone relates to Adderstone Hall near Belford where Lord Armstrong's great nephew and heir lived.

Ruthven, centre, was built around 1907 for shipbuilder William Wood of Wood and Skinner whose shipyard was at Bill Quay. The firm specialised in trawlers, colliers and small tramp steamers. Later residents included a paper merchant, and a Newcastle Town Clerk.

Shirley, bottom photograph, was built about 1903 for shipbuilder Richard Saxton White of Armstrong Whitworth & Co Ltd. He was a descendant of Sir William Henry White (1845-1913) reckoned to be one of the greatest naval architects of his day, instrumental in the foundation of the warship building yard at Elswick and on the board of directors of Swan Hunter and Wigham Richardson at the time of constructing the *Mauretania*. White Street in Low Walker is named after Sir W.H. White.

6. Jesmond Dean

For 65 years Jesmond Dean was either the home or later the town house of Sir William George Armstrong. There is little circumstantial evidence for the building and no photographs appear to exist. This drawing is undated. Land for the house and gardens had been provided by William Ramshaw, Armstrong's future father-in-law and owner of a successful engineering works at Bishop Auckland, to

celebrate his daughter's engagement. The couple married and moved into this 'modest but attractive' stone built dwelling in 1835.

The house was demolished in the mid 1920s and replaced by modern homes. Jesmond Dean lay approximately at the junction of Glastonbury Grove with Castleton Grove and, close by, there remains an oak tree planted alongside their drive on the couple's wedding day. Some of the stone from the house has been recycled to form the ground floors of two pairs of semi-detached homes in Glastonbury Grove.

On Jesmond Dene Road, there are three further links with the Armstrongs. The lodge at the corner of Lindisfarne Road once belonged to his agent, then two gate pillars further down the road, now part of a stone wall, once marked the entrance to their carriage-drive. Finally a bungalow even further down on the other side of the road, at an entrance into Jesmond Dene, was originally two separate cottages for servants.

7. The Banqueting Hall, c1883

By the late 1850s Jesmond Dean, the home of Sir William Armstrong, was proving too small and inconvenient for the entertainment of his growing number of business clients. John Dobson was engaged to design a purpose-built Banqueting Hall. Armstrong wanted his new building on a site, at that

time occupied by the Apple Tree Inn, on level ground just above the west bank of the Ouseburn and not far from his home. The Inn was moved to cottages nearby. The Banqueting Hall opened in 1862 followed by later extensions and then by a gatehouse higher up the hillside on Jesmond Dene Road in 1870.

The building featured tall windows and contained many statues. In an anteroom, many paintings were displayed alongside a hydraulic organ powered by water from a pond below what is now Paddy Freeman's lake in High Heaton. In 1883 the buildings and land formed part of Armstrong's gift to Newcastle Corporation. By 1977 substantial repairs had become necessary but they were never completed, and today the roofless Banqueting Hall serves as a workshop for stone masons.

The map is reproduced from the 1898 OS map and shows the layout of Armstrong's Jesmond Dean (spelled Dene here) house and the Banqueting Hall. The drawing, left, dates from the late 19th century. The unnamed buildings on the left, above the hospital site, belong to Jesmond Grove.

By 1898 Jesmond Dene Road, running north to south, parallel to the left of the Ouseburn, had reached its final form.

The drawing of the Banqueting Hall, left, dates from the late 19th century.

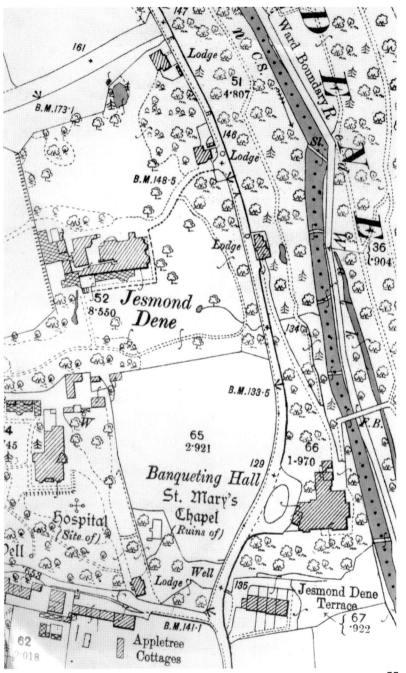

8. St Mary's Chapel, 1800s

St Mary's Chapel was a popular place of pilgrimage during the medieval period, attracting pilgrims to view holy relics possibly brought back from the Crusades by the Lords of Jesmond. Known at this time as The Blessed Mary of Jesmownt, pilgrims would have hoped to experience miracles associated with a nearby holy well.

After the chapel was dismantled in the 16th century, it had various owners, becoming a barn and a stable. Finally it came into the possession of Sir William Armstrong who gave the chapel and surrounding land to Newcastle Corporation for public access in 1883.

The chapel is the oldest ecclesiastical building in Newcastle with parts dating back to the early 12th century. Although roofless and a ruin, it continues to be used occasionally as a place of worship.

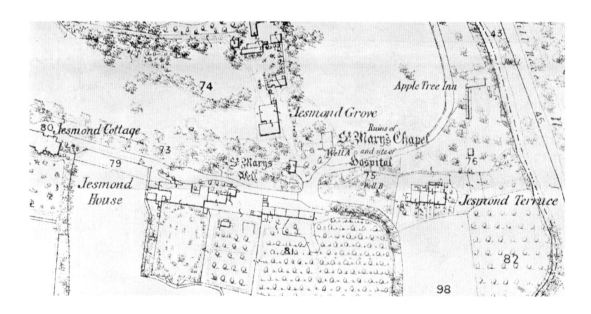

9. Jesmond Grove, 1919

This substantial mansion, was built for James Losh, barrister and Recorder of Newcastle, and served as the family home from around 1802 until his death some 30 years later. John Dobson is recorded as making alterations to the building in 1817.

Its position was to the west of St Mary's Chapel, overlooking a stream (the Moor Crook Letch) on land now laid out as Reid Park Road, which curves to follow the old Estate boundary wall.

Following James Losh's death occupants included a ship owner (George

Luckley) and a colliery owner (Henry Armstrong). William Bruce Reid, a local brewer, owned the property in the early 1900s. For several years before it was demolished in 1927 it functioned as a boarding house for pupils, and the head mistress, from Newcastle Church High School.

Although most of the Grove Estate was sold in 1927 for the building of modern homes, part of it was bought by the Church High School for a sports field. This playing field operated for over 40 years until being sold in the 1970s for further housing, now known as Reid Park Court and Reid Park Close.

The map, left, shows the layout of the Jesmond Grove Estate and the chapel from the first OS map of 1859. Jesmond Dene Road still has its double bend to give access to Jesmond Grove, Jesmond Cottage, and Jesmond Manor House. Jesmond Dene Road was straightened in 1871 (see page 14). The Apple Tree Inn is on the site which would become the Banqueting Hall.

10. Apple Tree Inn, 1882

The Apple Tree Inn originally stood on Jesmond Banks immediately above the west side of the Ouseburn in what is now Jesmond Dene. In 1860, it was forced to move following Sir William Armstrong's decision to build a Banqueting Hall on the same site. The Inn was relocated higher up the bankside to a stone cottage within old Jesmond village opposite St Mary's Chapel. With its red tiled roof, white washed walls and large garden of fruit trees, the Inn became a favourite haunt on a summer's evening where crowds would gather and 'refresh themselves either with luscious fruits, which the place provided, or perhaps the more usual alcoholic drinks'.

In the 1920s the Inn fell victim to a crackdown by magistrates who surprisingly decided this area of Jesmond had too many public houses. Shortly afterwards the area was totally cleared and replaced by residential housing.

The photograph shows the Inn behind the stone wall with one of two gate pillars visible belonging to Anderson's Drive (now known as The Grove) leading to their home at Jesmond Cottage. In the distance Jesmond Manor House is just visible. Today, the stone wall and both gate pillars remain at the lower end of Reid Park Road near to the junction with Jesmond Dene Road. The lodge, far right, has gone.

11. Jesmond Manor House, 1929

Jesmond Manor House and its gardens once stood at what is today the north end of Manor House Road. The site is now covered by parts of Grosvenor Avenue and Grosvenor Road.

The home of the Lords of the Manor of Jesmond stood here from at least the 12th century when it was given to Nicholas Grenville by Henry I. For most of this time the original village of Jesmond would have been close at hand with St Mary's Chapel at the other side of the nearby stream (the Moor Crook Letch).

All that survives from this once fine dwelling are the attractive wrought iron gates (in the foreground of the photograph) which were re-erected at Headlam Street as a feature of the 1970s Byker Wall development.

William Coulson, the son of a barber surgeon, and a wealthy merchant on the Quayside bought Jesmond Manor House in 1658 from a descendant of an earlier Lord of the Manor, the Anderson family, along with other land in Jesmond. The Coulsons rebuilt the house in 1720 and owned it and the surrounding land, until the early 19th century. In 1805 the land was sold to Sir Thomas Burdon and in 1809 the Manor House was sold to John Anderson (no relation to the earlier Andersons). Around a century later the house was 'much adorned and beautified'. A later owner of the house was Sir James Knott a local shipowner and founder of the Prince Line, one of the world's largest shipping lines. For a few years just before it was demolished, the house served as a home for nurses employed by the Ministry of Pensions.

12. St Mary's Well, 1920s

This well was at one time thought to have been the medieval well associated with the nearby chapel. It lies about 200m west of the chapel on the south bank of the Moor Crook Letch stream (culverted at this point) and near old Jesmond Village, but recent archaeology suggests this well dates from no earlier than the 17th Century and that it was a bathing place, perhaps even with a roof, for Jesmond Manor House just visible in the background of the photograph.

It is now believed the original holy well may have been nearer to the chapel, probably outside the east window, but it has left no trace.

Public access is about 200m along the Grove footpath from its junction with Reid Park Road, opposite the chapel.

13. Jesmond Cottage, Grove footpath, 1926

This Tudor style house was built for Matthew Anderson in 1831 on the site of an earlier dwelling. He was a ship-owner and general merchant who lived here for nearly 50 years. His initials and the date 1831, appear on the rainwater hoppers. The gate pillars, at the junction of his carriage drive (now a public footpath) with Reid Park Road, also date from this time.

After 1880, several families including David Adams, MP and ship owner lived here. This photograph of the house was taken when the Adams family were resident.

On the Grove footpath there is a lamp post outside the front door of the house which dates from 1930 when Adams was Lord Mayor of Newcastle.

From the mid-1940s, Akhurst Preparatory School occupied the building for over 60 years.

14. Grosvenor Villas, Grosvenor Road, c1910

Grosvenor Villas consists of four large double-fronted two-storey semi villas built in the late 1880s. They were some of the first houses in Grosvenor Road. These prestigious residences are set back slightly from the north side of the road in the form of a crescent with larger than average front gardens as well as a plot at the rear.

Little other construction work took place on this north side of Grosvenor Road at this time because the road formed the southern boundary of both Jesmond Manor House and Jesmond Cottage. After the demolition of the Jesmond Manor House in 1929, the land was sold, house building resumed and the road was completed over the next seven years or so. Meanwhile nursery gardens operated for a while on the site. Houses on the south side of Grosvenor Road were completed at a much earlier date.

The name Grosvenor has medieval French origins ('gros veneur') and became an English occupational surname relating to a chief huntsman. Such a person was often highly regarded during the Middle Ages and if successful usually rose rapidly up the peerage ladder.

15. Osborne Road, c1910

Standing prominently at the corner of Osborne Road and Acorn Road is Lloyds Bank, which has been on this site for over a century. Built as a private residence around 1893 the bank moved in about ten years later by initially sharing accommodation with the City Engineer (W.G. Laws) for a short while before his death in 1904. Lloyds eventually took over the whole house some five years later.

At a later date the left hand bay window became the present entrance door and then more recently cash machines have replaced the right hand bay window. The original house door is now a window.

This block of 1890s property between Acorn Road and Sanderson Road has attracted some of Newcastle's better known businessmen over the years including R. Sinclair the tobacco manufacturer, B. Pumphrey the grocer, W. Bookless the fruiterer as well as the architects J. Oswald and J.T. Cackett. Mrs J.J. Fenwick the widow of the department store founder also lived here for a few years.

Today, modern hotels occupy some of the houses with most of the remainder having been converted into apartments.

16. Acorn Road, 1971

A glimpse along Acorn Road from St George's Terrace. The vacant ground to the left had just been created by the demolition of houses on St George's Terrace for a Laws Stores Ltd. supermarket. A Tesco supermarket is there today.

Further along Acorn Road can be seen five shops completed around 1893, which are, today, a Chinese take-away, a seafood retailer, a gift shop, a hair salon and a jewellers' workshop and store. In 1968 the occupants were, in the same order, a radio supplies dealer, a fish-monger, a baker, a newsagents and a grocer. Shops on Acorn Road first appeared on the north (left) side around 1889 and were complete within 25 years. On the opposite side of the road shops materialised from around 1927 and were complete in under ten years.

17. St George's Terrace, 1910

The combined shops and dwellings on the west side of St George's Terrace, between Thornleigh Road and Coniston Avenue, were completed in 1900. They were the first buildings erected on this side of the road and in 1910 the shops were from left to right, a drapers, a creamery, ladies' outfitter, bakery, grocery and a

pharmacy. In the same order today there is a coffee house, post office and news agency, estate agency, pharmacy and wine shop. The remainder of this side of the road was completed by 1906 to include another ten shops, more terrace houses and two churches.

The two-storey terraced houses on the other side of the terrace were constructed earlier. Between Mistletoe Road and Acorn Road 28 homes were built 1882-1885, and were called Moor View. The houses from Acorn Road northwards, were built 1889-1900, to be eventually named St George's Terrace following the opening of nearby St George's Church in 1888. Moor View was re-named St George's Terrace in 1901. In 1971, five of the Victorian terraced houses at the corner of Acorn Road were demolished to make way for a small supermarket.

18. The United Methodist Free Church, and Jesmond Library, 1968

The United Methodist Free Church at the corner of Coniston Avenue, opened in 1901 to cope with Jesmond's ever increasing population. Before this date mission services and a Sunday School were held at the Co-op Hall in Fern Avenue. Designed by W.H. Knowles, the stone building contained a church hall and rooms for other activities. It had been hoped that a bigger church would be built on the adjoining site to the north.

Until 1963 Jesmond was the largest district in Newcastle without a permanent library. Some argued that it was 'a well informed population' and that a mobile library was more than sufficient. However in that year a small corner site in St George's Terrace became available and the proposal to build a library was agreed. The land had been owned by the adjacent Methodist Church and intended many years earlier for a larger church.

The architects Williamson, Faulkner-Brown & Partners then had the problem of how to squeeze a branch library (with nearly 18,000 books) into a mere 506 square yards and also how to blend the building with the varied surrounding structures. The answer was in a circular library almost fully glazed and with a serrated pattern that enabled direct sunlight to fall along the face of the book shelves. Behind the library lies the two-storey administration block.

Not only was the project completed on time with very few snags but the final cost of £33,623 was below the contract price. The library opened in 1963 and in 1965 the building received the RIBA bronze medal.

Some projecting stones that were intended to be keyed into the proposed extension can be seen on the gable end of the church.

19. St Hilda's church, c1910

St Hilda's Church on Thornleigh Road opened in 1905 as a daughter church of St George's on Osborne Road. Such had been the demand for seats at St George's, that 'once the bells had ceased, any vacant seats in rented pews were then available to waiting worshippers'. Also, following the creation of the West Jesmond Estate in the mid 1890s, several thousand more people were to be added to the parish.

Mr W.S. Hicks, the Diocesan Architect, was appointed and the Sunday school became the first building to be completed. It opened in 1900 and an inscription stone above a door in Thornleigh Road records the date. Original plans for the church had to be modified and in particular an attractive spire replaced a proposed tower. Finally a south aisle was added in 1909 to enable the building to qualify as a parish church.

This rather damaged photograph looks west along Thornleigh Road from St George's Terrace. St Hilda's is at the corner of Forsyth Road. In the distance Ashleigh Grove is visible on the other side of the railway beyond the railway sidings.

ST. GEORGE'S TERRACE, NEWCASTLE. 2697.

A view of the south end of St George's Terrace from the group of six shops opposite the end of Acorn Road, which branches off to the left.

The two-storey terraced houses in the background between Acorn Road and Mistletoe Road (in the distance) were the earliest in this terrace, having been built 1882-1885. They were known initially as Moor View because of their then uninterrupted view of the Town Moor, but renamed St George's Terrace in 1901.

A few properties on the opposite corner of Acorn Road (at the left of the photograph) were removed in 1971 to make way for a grocery store which has now become a small supermarket.

Jesmond, 1864

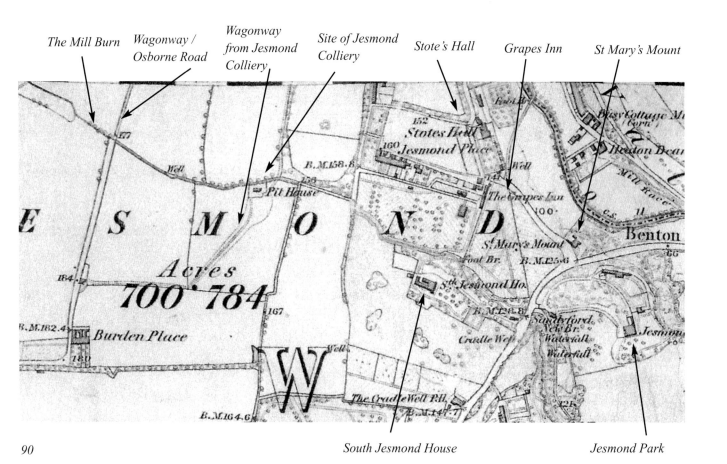

The Mill Burn

Wagonway / Osborne Road

Wagonway from Jesmond Colliery

Site of Jesmond Colliery

Stote's Hall

Grapes Inn

St Mary's Mount

South Jesmond House

Jesmond Park

Walk 4: From Haldane Court (site of Baptist Church), Osborne Road

1. Baptist Church (Haldane Court)
2. Osborne Road / Osborne Avenue
3. Osborne Road / Holly Avenue
4. Holly Medical Group
5. Osborne Road, Suffolk House
6. Larkspur Terrace
7. Osborne Road, St Margaret's Hotel
8. Cavendish Place
9. Stote's Hall

10. The Grapes Inn
11. Wellburn Park
12. St Mary's Mount
13. Jesmond Park
14. Rosebery Crescent
15. South Jesmond House
16. Fern Avenue Co-op
17. Osborne Avenue, pillar box

Jesmond, 1936

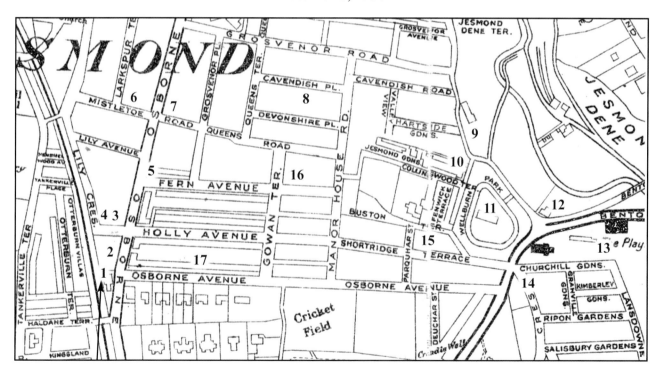

Start

1. Jesmond Baptist Church, Osborne Road, c1900

The top photograph looks north along Osborne Road towards the Baptist church which stood at the corner of Osborne Road and Haldane Terrace. The large house, Tyneholme, far right, has been replaced by part of the Nuffield Hospital and behind it can be seen the roof line of Burdon Place.

Burdon Place was built around 1810 as a small terrace housing speculation by Sir Thomas Burdon. Haldane Terrace, a later development, was named after Sir Thomas's great grandson Richard Burdon Haldane, who as an MP rose to become Viscount Haldane in 1911. The Burdon family were prominent non-conformists and actively supported the Baptist church which opened in 1887 to accommodate 700 people. Designed in the Norman style with a large square tower and short nave, it was regarded as unusual for this period. In 1973 Haldane Court, a sheltered housing development, replaced the church.

Horse-drawn trams were replaced by electric ones on this route in 1901.

Osborne Road, looking south around 1910. Beyond the massive square tower of the Baptist Church is the spire of the Methodist Church on Clayton Road.

2. Osborne Road, Osborne Avenue, 1930s

This postcard looks north along Osborne Road from its junction with Osborne Avenue towards the lofty bell tower of St George's Church in the distance.

Electric tram cars had been running on this route since the early 1900s and this particular tram is travelling north on either the 38 or 39 service from Central Station to the terminus at North Jesmond Avenue. Trams were replaced by trolley buses

Corner of Osborne Avenue, Newcastle-on-Tyne

on this route in September 1938. The dip in Osborne Road in the distance, at the Mistletoe Road and Queens Road junction, marks where the Mill Burn (fully culverted) flows beneath the road on its way from the Town Moor area to the Ouseburn.

The large house on the right is No.1 Osborne Avenue. It was built and occupied by William Temple, the builder of much of the housing between here and Acorn Road to the north. This house has some decorative and floral terracotta tiling on the gable end facing Osborne Road which records the date 1878. It is said that Temple's daughter, a keen botanist, successfully persuaded her father to name some of his new streets after shrubs, flowers or plants hence Acorn Road, Fern Avenue, Gowan Terrace, Holly Avenue, Larkspur Terrace, Lily Crescent and Avenue and Mistletoe Road. Later, Temple moved a short distance down Osborne Road to Tyneholme, an even larger mansion now demolished. The Nuffield Hospital occupies that site.

The remaining property visible on the photograph was completed before 1883 and has largely survived intact. At this date, the area beyond Acorn Road was classified as 'in the country'.

3. Osborne Road, Holly Avenue, c1910

Another view towards St George's Church from the junction with Holly Avenue (right foreground). Today, a century later, only the transport has changed, although the attractive Victorian iron railings around the front gardens disappeared nearly 70 years ago for the World War II effort.

The number 7 single deck electric tram is on its way from the Central Station to the terminus further along Osborne Road at North Jesmond Avenue. This type of tram, dark maroon in colour, began service in 1902 with seating for 37 on long wooden benches facing each other and with a separate compartment for smokers. Electric trolleybuses served this route from 1938 until motorbuses took over in 1965.

The houses on the right date from c1879 and consist of a row of six double fronted substantial terraced homes (as far as Fern Ave) with an open stone porch to the front door. They are white brick, two storeys high with attics, and attractive wrought iron work over the ground floor bay windows. Occupants at the time of the photograph included a French consul, an enamelled slate manufacturer, a coal owner, a physician and a solicitor. On the opposite side of Osborne Road the red brick houses are similarly large and a few years later in date.

4. Holly Medical Group, c1910

This range of houses on Osborne Road, between Holly Avenue West (foreground) and Lily Avenue, were completed around 1882 to become the homes of local business and professional people. After World War II they were gradually divided up into flats and apartments.

An exception is the corner property in the foreground which has a stone feature on its gable end – the rod of Asclepius (the Greek God of Medicine) entwined with a serpent, which is associated with the power of healing because of its ability to rejuvenate by shedding its skin every year. This feature is the international medical symbol as well as the emblem of the NHS. It is hidden behind a tree in the photograph.

Although the first occupier of this corner house was an engineer, the first of several medical practitioners arrived a few years later and it has remained a doctors' surgery ever since. It is known today as the Holly Medical Group.

5. Osborne Road, Suffolk House, c1895

Suffolk House, as it came to be known, was built around 1882 as a ladies' private school at the corner of Osborne Road and Fern Avenue. It occupied, it was said, 'a charming situation in one of the healthiest suburbs of Newcastle within a few minutes walk of the Moor and Jesmond Dene, and convenient of access from the city by tram-cars passing the school every ten minutes'.

The school, which included boarders, catered for 'the education of girls up to the highest requirements of the University curricula and of refined society'. In addition, because the principal's daughter was a champion tennis player, pupils could 'enjoy the special advantages in tuition from so accomplished a player'.

After about 20 years the school closed and later owners have included a ship owner, solicitor and cashier. The Gregg High School for girls occupied the building from around 1960. Today the premises function as apartments for students.

6. Larkspur Terrace, c1910

A view of the west side of Larkspur Terrace from Mistletoe Road, looking north towards Acorn Road. These 60 or so white brick houses were completed in the 1880s. They all have ground floor bay windows and neat front gardens behind decorative iron railings together with attractive wooden porch hoods, pedimented format, over the front door. The building project was one of several thoroughfares in Jesmond master-minded by William Temple, the builder, and named after either plants, flowers or shrubs apparently at the request of his daughter, a keen botanist. The original garden railings and cobble-stones disappeared many years ago.

7. Osborne Road and St Margaret's Hotel, c1910

This block of private dwellings in Osborne Road between Queen's Road (foreground) and Grosvenor Road was built in the early to mid 1880s.

St Margaret's Boarding House opened around 1912 within the three properties nearest Queen's Road. The advertisement, right, is dated 1929. It later became St Margaret's Temperance Hotel, St Margaret's Private Hotel, and the Avon Hotel in the 1960s. Meanwhile, four adjacent houses were converted into 'The Methodist International House'.

Today a large modern hotel has taken over the former Avon and Methodist House and in doing so has substantially altered their appearance. The gothic style attics have been replaced by a continuous line of modern bedroom attic windows, most doors have been replaced by windows and the chimney stacks and gardens have disappeared.

Most of the remaining private houses south of Grosvenor Road have now also been converted into hotels.

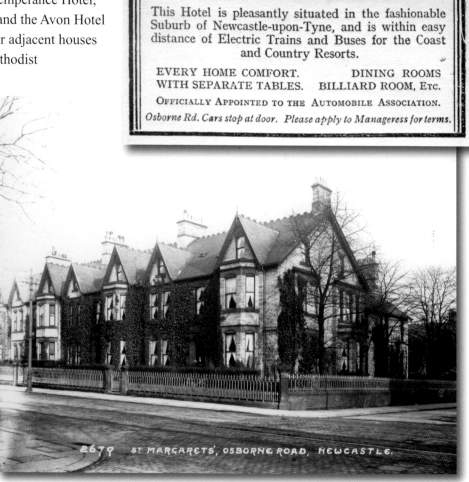

Telegrams:
"St. Margarets, Osborne Rd., Newcastle."

Telephone:
453 Jesmond.

St. Margaret's Hotel

64 to 68 OSBORNE ROAD, JESMOND, NEWCASTLE-UPON-TYNE.

This Hotel is pleasantly situated in the fashionable Suburb of Newcastle-upon-Tyne, and is within easy distance of Electric Trains and Buses for the Coast and Country Resorts.

EVERY HOME COMFORT.   DINING ROOMS
WITH SEPARATE TABLES.   BILLIARD ROOM, Etc.

OFFICIALLY APPOINTED TO THE AUTOMOBILE ASSOCIATION.

Osborne Rd. Cars stop at door. Please apply to Manageress for terms.

2679 ST MARGARETS, OSBORNE ROAD, NEWCASTLE.

8. Cavendish Place, 1910

A view of Cavendish Place taken from Manor House Road towards Queens Terrace. When completed, around 1901, these were houses 'to meet the requirements of the families of respectable workmen and members of the lower middle class'. All the houses had 'the latest conveniences, overshot roofs and superior bay window masonry'. Each house contained six, seven or nine rooms and in their front rooms there were substantial carved oak mantelpieces 'a luxury formerly confined to elaborate mansions'.

William Cavendish (1592-1676), 1st Duke of Newcastle, was one of the richest men in England and a leading Royalist general during the English Civil War. A Yorkshireman by birth, some of his enormous wealth came from his Northumbrian mother (Catherine Ogle) who had inherited vast estates in Northumberland including a third of Jesmond. As commander of the Royalist army north of the River Trent, which he largely funded, he was given the task among others, of securing Newcastle against the Parliamentary troops. His reward was a dukedom. His financial assistance cost him a staggering £941,000 (17th century prices)! Other local street names connected with the Cavendish family are Devonshire, Welbeck, Portland and Bentinck.

9. Stote's Hall, 1957

Stote's Hall stood above Jesmond Dene, set back from Jesmond Dene Road, nearly opposite the entrance to Collingwood Terrace where the coachman's cottage remains.

There was probably a farmhouse on this site by at least the 15th century which was then rebuilt by the Gibson family around 1600. Above the front door was a stone plaque dated 1607 together with the Arms of the Newcastle Merchant Adventurers Guild to which they belonged. Subsequently many alterations and extensions to the building took place.

In 1650 it is said to have been the resting place of Oliver Cromwell on his way to Scotland. Later, Sir Richard Stote, a London lawyer, bought the house. Dr Charles Hutton, a local mathematician and fellow of the Royal Society opened a school here in the 18th century and one of his pupils, John Scott, husband of Bessie Surtees, eventually became Lord Chancellor of England and finally Lord Eldon.

During World War II, the house became an Air Raid Precautions depot and suffered bomb damage when its adjacent lodge was destroyed. It was demolished in the 1950s and Jesmond Dene extended for public access leaving behind only a few trees and traces of garden terracing on the steep slopes. This photograph was taken by Newcastle photographer Jimmy Forsyth shortly before demolition. The plaque above the doorway can clearly be seen.

10. The Grapes Inn

The Grapes Inn was located around the middle of the present day Fenwick Terrace and appears to have existed from at least the late 1700s until 1864. Initially known as the Rosetree it is uncertain when the name changed.

A local author writing in 1801 paints a glowing account of this area: 'To Jesmond on a summer morning is one of the sweetest walks in the vicinity of Newcastle. If this pleasant village has lost its beauty it is amply compensated for by the improvements made there especially in that little spot of ground occupied by Mr Dewar as a common garden. By his industry and unwearied attention this has improved to such a degree of perfection as to enable him to support a large family in a comfortable manner. Although it does not contain two acres of land it is now so much resorted to as a place of recreation during the summer that the visitors are agreeably accommodated with tea, cider, etc as well as with the most delicious fruits in season'.

Another writer, some 20 years later comments that the property was 'extended by the removal of an unseemly pit heap and the whole area brought into a surprising state of order and fruitfulness, producing an abundance of delicious fruits for the refreshment of the numerous parties who visit this delightful spot.'

In 1864 the Inn and adjoining public nursery gardens, by this time covering five acres, were sold for the building of Orchard House, Fenwick Terrace and Collingwood Terrace. The adjacent Jesmond Gardens (formerly Jesmond Place) goes back much earlier to around 1820, as one of the earliest residential developments in Jesmond.

This sketch is undated. The unusual stone entrance pillars have been recreated in a similar style at the Jesmond Dene Road entrance to this small residential estate.

11. Wellburn, 1920s

In 1879 William Henry Holmes, a Quaker and founder of the Stepney Paint Works in Shieldfield, bought a four acre field near to the west end of the recently opened Armstrong bridge to have a substantial villa built for himself and family. Frank Rich, who lived close by in Jesmond Gardens, designed the mansion which included 15 rooms at ground floor level with ten bedrooms above, including attics for the servants. The property was named Wellburn, a name said to have been contrived from the nearby Cradle Well and the Mill Burn. At one time a windmill stood in the four acre field.

John Henry Holmes, the son of William, set up an Electrical Engineering business in Shieldfield, that became world famous for various electrical innovations including the quick-break light switch. In 1883 Wellburn became the first private house in Newcastle to be lit by electricity.

Wellburn was demolished around 1931 and replaced by an estate of mainly semi-detached homes, Wellburn Park. Apart from sections of stone wall which had enclosed the original villa and grounds nothing remains of the building. Fortunately most of Holmes' electrical workshop has been preserved and is on view at Newcastle's Discovery Museum.

12. St Mary's Mount, 1920s

This 'snug villa', later known as St Mary's Mount, was built shortly before 1828 for the retirement that year of the Rev. Edward Moises, headmaster of the Royal Grammar School. Having lived on the school premises for 41 years, Moises just wanted 'to live in the country at Jesmond' for the remainder of his life. The school buildings at Westgate had in former times been the medieval Hospital of St Mary the Virgin and conveniently the land for the proposed house at Jesmond was also owned by the Hospital.

St Mary's Mount lay on the opposite side of Benton Bank to Jesmond Park – the relatively recently built country mansion of Armorer Donkin, a well-known local solicitor, and not too far away from the Armstrongs (father and son) who arrived a few years later. Moises continued to live here with his two daughters for another 17 years until his death in 1845 aged 82.

Later occupants of St Mary's Mount included various merchants and for a period of 45 years the owners were the Coxon family whose department store stood at the corner of Market Street and Grey Street.

The property was demolished in the early 1970s following its use as kennels by a breeder of dogs. Today the site has been landscaped and is at the junction of Jesmond Dene Road and Benton Bank at the west end of Armstrong Bridge, opened 1878.

Reproduced from In Trust magazine, 1984

Wellburn is the house just visible on the extreme lower left of this 1920s photograph. St Mary's Mount is at the junction of Jesmond Road and Benton Bank just as the road splits off towards Armstrong Bridge opposite Holy Trinity Church. The map on page 107 helps to identify the buildings.

Heaton Dene House, now demolished, is top left, with Colman's Field to the right.

Top right, on Benton Bank, is a theatre built in 1921, which was first called the Jesmond Kursaal, then the Jesmond Pavilion, and then the Dinky until 1928 when it was enlarged to become the Playhouse. It was demolished in 1971.

13. Jesmond Park, 1884

This large villa, set in spacious grounds, was built in 1826 for Armorer Donkin, the successful local solicitor.

This drawing dates from around 1843.

Double-fronted and south-facing, overlooking the Ouseburn Valley, it contained 'large lofty rooms and numerous bedrooms'. Other buildings on the eight acre site included servants' houses, stables, byres, coach houses, offices and a lodge at the Jesmond Road entrance near Sandyford New Bridge over the Mill Burn. Donkin, a bachelor, was famed for his generous hospitality which attracted local as well as national celebrities such as William Cobbett, the politician and journalist, and Leigh Hunt the poet and essayist.

Following Donkin's death in 1851 all of his estate, by this time over 30 acres, was left to William George Armstrong his former pupil and later business partner. Later occupiers of the property included a corn merchant, iron founder, physician and banker.

The mansion was demolished in 1899 and replaced by an estate of mainly brick terraced houses built mostly between 1903 and 1909. The thoroughfares were named after prominent British statesmen of that time and known as 'Gardens' in all but one case. Kimberley Gardens stands approximately on the site of the mansion with Churchill Gardens running almost parallel to the carriage drive from Jesmond Road.

The illustration below featured in the *Illustrated London News*, August 16, 1884 which covered the visit of the Prince and Princess of Wales to open Jesmond Dene, the Hancock Museum and the Albert Edward Dock at Coble Dene. Jesmond Park is the large villa to the far left. In the foreground is Armstrong Park and Armstrong Bridge is beyond. The royal party is to the right, travelling towards Jesmond Dene for the opening ceremony.

14. Rosebery Crescent, c1910

This photograph, taken near the northern end of Rosebery Crescent, shows some of the earliest houses built on the former Jesmond Park estate around 1903. In the distance is a temporary iron church (with spire) installed about 1905 to enable services to continue pending the collection of further funds necessary for the completion of the intended Holy Trinity Church. At this time only the east end or chancel, had been built. Seventeen years later, in 1922, the building was completed as the 'War Memorial Church of the Holy Trinity', largely owing to the generosity of R.S. Dalgliesh, a Newcastle shipowner and later Lord Mayor. Appropriately the weather vane on top of the spire is shaped like a ship. Originally planned as a daughter church of Jesmond Parish Church and St George's Parish Church, Holy Trinity became a separate parish in 1926.

Most of the houses featured in the photograph were demolished in preparation for the construction of the Cradlewell Bypass and viaduct in the 1990s. The Bypass is partly beneath where the houses once stood and today there is a landscaped area of grass and trees above the Bypass.

The Crescent was named after Lord Rosebery the former Liberal Prime Minister, who at 47 years of age, succeeded W.E. Gladstone in 1894. Lord Rosebery was a 'noted racehorse owner' having won the Derby on three occasions.

15. South Jesmond House, 1894

First known as the Minories, the mansion was probably built in the late 1830s for William Armstrong, commission agent and corn merchant, the father of Lord Armstrong. William Armstrong had moved here from his 'modest terrace house' in Pleasant Row, Shieldfield Green. Part of the attraction in moving here must have been that his son was living nearby at Jesmond Dean and his close friend, Armorer Donkin, was only a few hundred yards away at Jesmond Park.

No photograph exists of the villa. However, this 1894 map (enlarged) illustrates the extent of the estate with

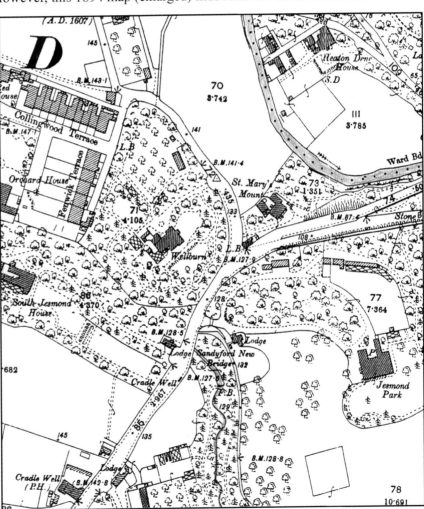

the Mill Burn, culverted at this point, running alongside the carriage-drive before flowing beneath Sandyford New Bridge (now beneath Jesmond Road).

Around 1902, the property was bought by Robert Deuchar, brewer and property speculator, who replaced the mansion and the rest of the estate with brick terraced housing. Streets were given names associated with Deuchar namely Shortridge and Buston Terraces and Farquhar Street. For the last ten years of Deuchar's life he lived at Shortridge Hall close to High Buston near Warkworth and after his death his eldest son Farquhar carried on the family business. Deuchar Street is nearby. Interestingly, the only thoroughfares named as 'streets' in Jesmond are Farquhar Street and Deuchar Street.

16. Fern Avenue Co-op, c1900

Many Co-operative branches opened in Newcastle during the late Victorian period with the Fern Avenue branch opening around 1898. The photograph shows the cobbled streets of Gowan Terrace to the left and Fern Avenue to the right. Fern Avenue was gradually built up from the late 1870s, starting at the Osborne Road end, with the south side being largely completed within ten years. The north side took longer and the houses to the right of the picture, next to the Co-op building, were not completed until around 1907.

The substantial brick building consisted of a grocery shop on the ground floor with a hall above for social events. A stone lintel above an entrance is engraved CO-OPERATIVE HALL. An application to use the hall for public dancing in the early days was rejected because it may have led to 'promiscuous dancing'. For a year or two the United Methodist Free Church held their services here until their new church at St George's Terrace opened in 1901. In 1914, when the army took over West Jesmond School, the Co-op was occupied by part of the

school for several months. A Masonic Lodge has met on the upper floor since 1923.

Before the Co-op development in the 1890s this site was the home of the Avenues Lawn Tennis Club for seven years. Founded in 1883 by members of Jesmond Wesleyan Church, which included Mr J.J. Fenwick, founder of the department store, the club played on two rented grass courts (later cemented). In 1890 the club moved to new premises on Osborne Road. Jesmond Colliery occupied the site from a much earlier date (see introduction).

17. The Penfold pillar box, Osborne Avenue

The oldest pillar box in Newcastle stands in Osborne Avenue. Installed in 1884 and known as a 'Penfold', it is distinctive by being six-sided and ornate on top, with acanthus leaves and beads. J.W. Penfold, a Post Office consulting engineer, was commissioned in 1864 to improve the appearance of the original and rather plain cylindrical pillar box. However, the 'Penfold' had a limited life span, largely due to it being more expensive to produce and maintain as well as having internal construction problems resulting in mail becoming trapped. A return was made to the more practicable less decorated cylindrical shape.

Anthony Trollope, a Post Office surveyor – later to receive fame as a novelist – had been sent to the Channel Islands in 1851 in response to the public's demand to follow the Continent's example of providing roadside collection boxes. The result was the UK's first pillar box situated at St Helier (Jersey) in 1852, followed a year later by the first mainland pillar box at Carlisle, from where they spread across Britain. Initially these cast iron pillar boxes were painted dark green until, several years later, red was considered more appropriate. The pillar box proved to be a cheaper alternative than the opening of additional and expensive 'Letter Receiving Offices' which had been the norm before the advent of the popular Penny Post pre-payment system in 1840.

Jesmond, 1864

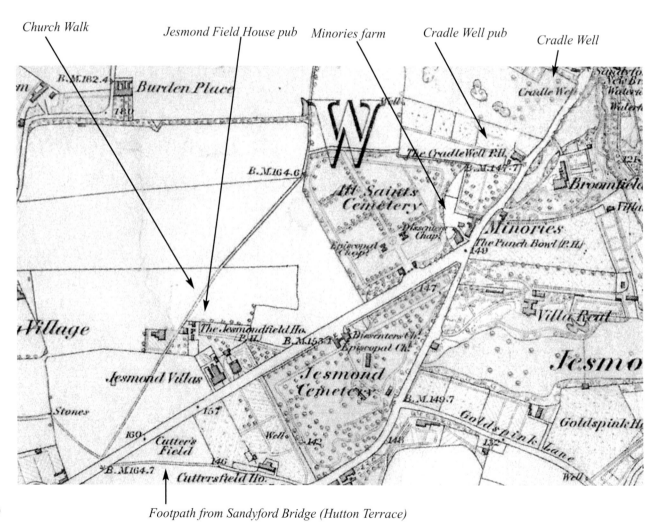

Church Walk
Jesmond Field House pub
Minories farm
Cradle Well pub
Cradle Well
Footpath from Sandyford Bridge (Hutton Terrace)

Walk 5: From the junction of Jesmond Road with Osborne Road

1. Osborne Road
2. Mansion House
3. The Willows
4. Cricket Ground
5. Cradle Well Pub

6. Minories House
7. All Saints Cemetery
8. Jesmond Old Cemetery
9. Imperial Hotel

Jesmond, 1936

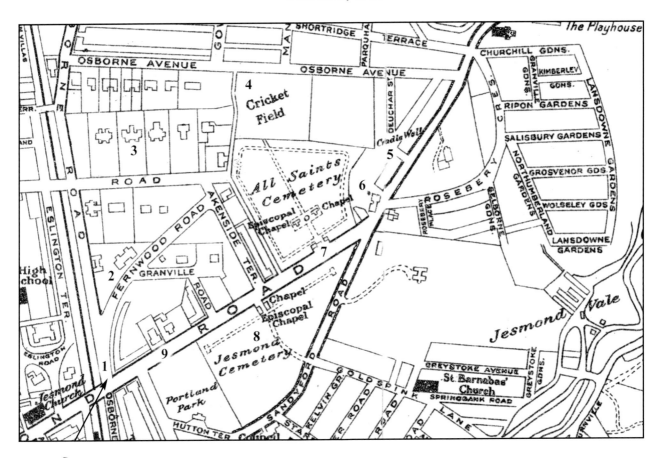

1. Nos. 1-6 Osborne Road, 1968

Standing majestically at the south end of Osborne Road near its junction with Jesmond Road is a stylish row of six spacious double-fronted houses built during the mid 1870s. This photograph features four of these homes, from right to left, No. 3 (only half the dwelling) then Nos. 4, 5 and 6. In the distance to the left behind the trees is the Mansion House in Fernwood Road.

Built as superior residences for professional persons (surgeons, lawyers, ship-owners) the houses all became private hotels at various times during the 1920s. Following the end of World War II, Nos. 1 and 2 became regional offices for the Ministry of Health and other government agencies, no. 3 contained a commercial college, Nos. 4 and 5 continued as an hotel and No. 6 was in use as a nurses' home. Today the buildings operate either as offices or, as in the case of Nos. 4, 5 and 6 with the modern attics, as an 'aparthotel'.

2. The Mansion House, 1967

This substantial Victorian villa in Fernwood Road, known as Thurso House, is the City's Mansion House. It replaced an earlier Mansion House in Ellison Place. Centuries ago the role of the Mansion House was to provide an official residence for the mayor and also for the Judges of the Assize but today this is no longer the case and the building's main use is for civic functions and receptions.

It became the Mansion House through the generosity of Sir Arthur Munro Sutherland who bequeathed his home to the city at his death in 1953. He wrote 'It is a lovely home and I hope it will prove worthy of the city of my birth'. Sir Arthur's grandfather, Benjamin, had arrived in the early 1800s from Thurso (in the north of Scotland) as a boot and shoe maker and as the family prospered his son, Benjamin John, became a shipping merchant. It was Benjamin John who acquired the three-year-old property in 1879 which at that time consisted of two adjoining identical houses. The Sutherlands lived in Thurso House while the other villa, Kelso House, was rented to business associates. Eventually both villas were consolidated into one and shortly afterwards Sir Arthur, son of Benjamin John, took possession to create a lavish town house.

Often described as the last of Tyneside's merchant princes, Sir Arthur had become a wealthy shipowner with a deep interest in civic affairs which led to his election as Lord Mayor of Newcastle in 1918 followed by a knighthood two years later.

3. The Willows, Clayton Road East, c1910

This substantial semi villa in Clayton Road East, known as The Willows, dates from around 1876. It was the home of Sir George Burton Hunter, shipbuilder and philanthropist, for 47 years until his death in 1937. Hunter was instrumental in the merger of Swan & Hunter with J. Wigham Richardson to form the powerful company, Swan Hunter and Wigham Richardson, that successfully bid for the contract to build the *Mauretania*, the world's largest and fastest luxury ocean liner when launched in 1906.

His next door neighbour for many years at Holmwood was Thomas Hudson Bainbridge, second of Emerson Muschamp Bainbridge's 15 children. For 20 years Thomas managed Bainbridge's department store (now John Lewis), founded by his father. Both the Hunter and Bainbridge families were committed Methodists.

Other prominent local businessmen lived on Clayton Road East including William Stewart the tea merchant, Sir Walter Runciman owner of the Moor Shipping Line and James Skinner, another shipbuilder.

Some of these grand Victorian houses have been replaced by new buildings. A few remain in private hands.

4. Northumberland County Cricket Club, c1950

Northumberland County Cricket Club acquired the compact Osborne Avenue Ground (nearly 3.5 acres) in 1897, with financial assistance, said to be in the region of £7,000, provided by some 'influential gentlemen'. The club formed in 1881 to play representative and county games, without a ground of their own. Home matches were played elsewhere including Gosforth (South Northumberland), Tynemouth (Preston Lane) and Heaton Lane (now Road). This ground sharing caused problems, particularly with fixtures, poor attendances and even a reluctance to play for the county which all contributed to much financial anxiety.

Shortly after settling at their new Jesmond ground, several extensions and improvements took place including the transfer of a replica Swiss Chalet from the Queen Victoria Jubilee Exhibition of 1887, held on the Town Moor, to become the pavilion (far left in the photograph). This recycled chalet was replaced in 1963 by a purpose-built pavilion.

The Northumberland County Cricket Club is not to be confused with the older Northumberland Cricket Club that played at Bath Road (now Northumberland Road) from 1839 until 1881 then at Heaton Road until its demise in 1899. They were a private club and despite their name, were never representative of the County of Northumberland for cricket.

5. The Cradle Well, 1890s

The original Cradle Well consisted of three stone troughs in the shape of a cradle together with an attached iron ladle. It once stood beside Benton Lane (now Jesmond Road) near New Sandyford Bridge close to the present junction with Osborne Avenue where a replica is now situated.

The Cradle Well pub stood near to the well and first appeared in the directories of 1833. The well was a popular venue during the 19th century for publicans to obtain 'pure water to mix spirits with' and for the general public to 'drink fresh spring water'.

Around 1903 road improvements took place which involved the culverting of the nearby Mill Burn, the removal of the bridge, as well as the widening and straightening of the thoroughfare which resulted in the demise of the old pub and well. Robert Deuchar who had recently taken over the South Jesmond Estate opened the present Cradle Well pub in 1904. The old stone Cradle Well was removed to nearby Armstrong Park where the remains can still be seen close to King John's Well.

6. Minories House, Jesmond Road, 1971

Minories House, a double-fronted two-storey dwelling with decorated ironwork above the bay windows, was built around 1855 for a family of pawnbrokers. They continued to live on this prominent site at the junction of Jesmond Road and Sandyford Road until about 1920. Later, an extension was added following the conversion of the building into a joinery workshop and office. When this photograph was taken the building was a works department for Newcastle City Council. It has now been modernised into student accommodation.

Before the 1850s Minories Farm occupied this site, with over 40 acres of fields extending as far west as Brandling Place. Attached to the farm buildings was the old Punch Bowl pub which was replaced by the present building in 1878. All this land was owned by James Archbold, a local businessman and former mayor of Newcastle. Nearby Archbold Terrace is named after him.

Several buildings in this area have, at one time or another, adopted the word 'Minories' as part of their name. The word is associated with Franciscan friars, also known as the Friars Minor (little brethren) because of their extreme humility while caring for the poor and sick (particularly lepers). It is possible that a religious building did once exist in this area, perhaps connected with the Franciscans (or Grey Friars) who from around 1260 had a Friary close to the Pilgrim Gate in Newcastle, but so far no site in Jesmond has been identified. In medieval days the Mary Magdalene Hospital for lepers was nearby at Barras Bridge, and St Mary's Chapel and Well, near the Manor House, were not far away.

7. All Saints Cemetery, 1971

All Saints municipal cemetery opened in 1857 on the opposite side of Cemetery Road (later Jesmond Road) to the privately owned Jesmond Old Cemetery. It replaced All Saints churchyard in central Newcastle following the closure by Act of Parliament, of all urban parish churchyards. Municipal cemeteries had the major advantage over churchyards of being much larger in size and also that they catered for all religions. Large scale residential housing appeared around the cemetery at a later date.

Because the threat from grave robbers had passed well before this date, cast iron railings with fleur-de-lys heads were considered adequate to enclose the area instead of the nine feet high stone wall which protected Jesmond Old Cemetery. The cemetery was extended to Osborne Avenue in the early 1900s, on land known as Dead Men's Graves and a pedestrian gate opened to that thoroughfare. Nearly 90,000 burials have taken place to date. John Green, a noted Newcastle architect, designed the cemetery and its fine Gothic gateway.

Samuel Smith the founder of Rington's tea, Mark Toney the ice cream manufacturer and Alex Gardner captain of Newcastle United during their glory years before World War I are all buried here.

8. Jesmond Old Cemetery, c1900

Jesmond Old Cemetery opened in 1836 as a privately owned 11-acre cemetery to the design of architect John Dobson. Although it was more expensive to be buried here, it nevertheless proved for some to be a popular alternative to the ancient urban parish churchyards which tended to be relatively small, overcrowded and were Church of England. The advantages of a private cemetery were that they catered for all religions, were more spacious and tranquil, offered freehold plots and lockable gates as well as providing, in this case, a high surrounding wall to deter potential grave robbers who were prevalent at this time.

The need for private cemeteries largely decreased after the 1850s owing to the establishment of municipal cemeteries. Today, this burial ground is also managed and owned by Newcastle Council rather than by the directors and shareholders of a private company. Interments still take place here and to date total about 25,000.

The photograph illustrates the fine classical North Gate, as seen from a rather muddy Jesmond Road with chapels on either side of the entrance. Catacombs exist beneath the buildings. These structures, both above and below ground, are currently occupied either by archaeologists or their equipment.

This is the last resting place of many Tyneside celebrities including John Dobson the architect and the department store founders Emerson Muschamp Bainbridge and John James Fenwick.

ʓ. Imperial Hotel, Jesmond Road c1910, 1967

The Imperial Hotel opened in 1903 in one of a row of six large private dwellings known as Jesmond Villas. Dating from the 1840s these homes were among the earliest residences in Jesmond and stood immediately in front of the older Jesmond Field House pub (replaced by the Granville Court flats) that lay alongside the old Church Walk 'Foot Road' to Jesmond village from Newcastle. By the 1910s, the hotel had expanded into two more villas and was known as the Imperial Temperance Hotel. The houses on either side of the Villas were completed before 1880.

The Imperial Hotel in 1967.

During the 1930s the Embassy Residential Hotel, replaced the three remaining Jesmond Villas and a few decades later both hotels merged to create an enlarged Imperial Hotel. Later, the Embassy building was demolished and the Imperial Hotel expanded its facilities.

Some of the original architectural features in the photograph have been retained whilst others such as the entrance veranda, railings and gate pillars have disappeared. Also note the tram lines on Jesmond Road.